Dry Grass Whispering

*by
Norah Kersh*

Copyright © Norah Kersh 2010
Published by Norah Kersh

ISBN 978 0 9579285 1 0
First published 2010
First edition

This book is copyright apart from any fair dealing for the purpose of private research, criticism or review, as permitted under the copyright act, no part may be reproduced by any process without the written permission of the author.

*Dedicated
to my beloved family*

iv

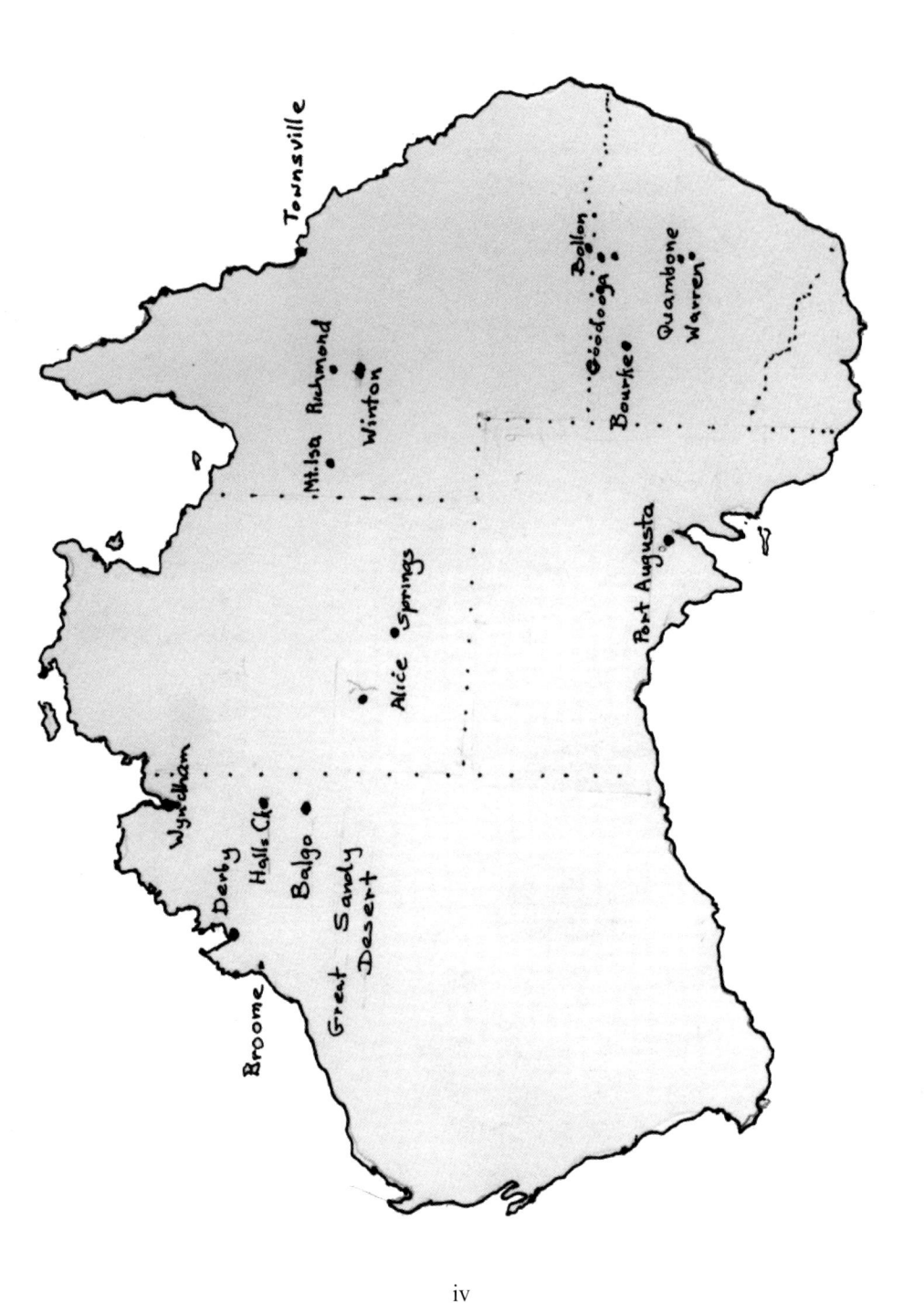

Contents

Acknowledgement	vii
Foreword	ix
Splashed with sunlight	1
Golden Fleece	8
Fairy Floss and Boxing Troupe	14
Open Doors	17
Boarding School	19
Loreto	22
Coming Home	25
Jackaroo	31
Gypsies	35
From Woolerina to Goodooga	39
Travelling West	43
Balgo Mission	48
Our Early Days at Balgo	63
Wedding at Gordon Downs	70
Brendan's Arrival	73
To the Alice for Peter	81
Droving Cattle	86
My Sister Betty	91
Building the Homestead	94
Across the Airwaves – Neighbours	98
Memories Unwrapped	100
Bushfires and Other Hazards	106
Going East	109
Wings over the Spinifex	111
No Room for Luxury Items – Life in the Stock Camp	115
Cattle Rush	118

She Won't Make it	122
Social Event of the Year	126
Homecoming	132
Going to Bora	138
Areas of Blowing Dust	151
One Wet Season	155
S.O.T.A. School of the Air	158
Shearing	165
Cathedral	170
Gone Missing	175
Tyler's Story	178
A Patchwork	185
Epilogue - My Beautiful Wild Son	192

Acknowledgements

My heartfelt thanks to all who have helped me along the journey:

To Conor, for instigating this whole saga.

To Bernadette, who, by way of the magic memory stick, willingly and repeatedly transferred the script south.

To Jenny and Ken Oats, VISE teachers who were helping my grandchildren at Bora. When first I put biro to exercise book, Jenny typed and Ken printed my essays into legible form.

To Michael Perfrement for introducing me to the mysteries of a laptop.

To John for, when my memory flagged, supplying nuts and bolts information,.

To my gracious sister, Fran Spora, who read and commented most helpfully as the story took shape. To my sister Bernie Mullany for your kindly vote of confidence.

To Fiona Inglis, who initially contacted me regarding this story; your gracious encouragement has been invaluable. And to Sarah Murdoch, who suggested to Fiona that I might have a story to tell.

To Jan Hutchinson for your editing advice and enjoyable telephone conversations.

To my brother Mike for your heart-warming contribution.

To Tony Stokes for his careful proofreading.

To Rosana for designing the book cover and for your photo taken at sundown between Julia Creek and Cloncurry.

To Father Frank Brennan: Thank you for making time to read the manuscript and to write the Foreword. I am most grateful.

Most of all, to my beautiful children, without whom there would be no story.

Foreword
to
Dry Grass Whispering

Norah was one of eleven children in the O'Brien family. She had only one brother and attended girls' boarding schools. She and John Kersh raised a family of seven boys and two girls. She is a no nonsense country girl who has seen it all, and never overstates the case or her emotions. As a child she was happy, being always encouraged by parents "to have opinions and ask questions". By the time she comes to describe the births of her own children she says, "Quentin, Joe and Rosana were born into our family. Only a line here, though each one an epic."

She fell head over heels for John, the handsome jackaroo from the city: "On meeting John, my dreams of Jim were blown away. I was smitten. This new jackaroo wasn't just a pretty face; he was capable and interesting." She was devastated by their separation: "Separation was a challenge! At the end of this dry year there was no sign of wet and no early storms." Meanwhile they raised a robustly independent family living in places as remote as Balgo Hills in the east Kimberley and Bora and Cathedral Stations, out of Winton, North Queensland.

Balgo was established as a Catholic Aboriginal mission in 1939. John and Norah arrived there in 1967, the year of the referendum* which delivered funds and the national spotlight to such places for the first time. As they crossed Australia, they "camped under the stars, one night gazing at an eclipse

---

* *Equal citizen rights for Aboriginal people.*

of the moon". She wrote in her diary: "Came into real desert – mile upon mile raw red Spinifex covered sand." She says, "The lights of Balgo were like a miracle in the desert." It was fashionable to claim that the only whites in these places were missionaries, madmen or mercenaries. The Kersh family fitted none of those moulds. They lived as poor as church mice. Norah stayed in the Aboriginal Children's hostel in Derby when she went to town to give birth. She was no missionary though she has always been a woman of strong and simple faith, admiring those missionaries who did come with nothing other than their generous spirits and love for the poorest and most marginalised. When a child, her family would rotate between Quambone and Marthaguy Creek NSW to attend weekly mass: "God was loving and bountiful as far as I was concerned. He came with billy tea at Marthaguy Hall". She has known family tragedy ever since the drowning of her six year old niece on Boxing Day when she was young girl home from boarding school. She has kept very grounded and sane whether in Balgo or Balmain: "It is often said of country people that distance doesn't matter to us. Distance is what we do." Distance is what helps them survive, maintaining their own independence and vision whatever the prevailing fads and orthodoxies of the city.

She and the family spent seven years at Balgo "at the tail end of a period when the old ways for both tribal people and Kimberley station people in general, was changing." When they left, they bought their first cattle property, "Bora 'walk in walk out' with 8000 sheep for which we could wait till after shearing before paying." As the children grew up, they all had their scrapes enjoying near escapes with motor bikes and snakes. Joe aged 17 collided with a truck in Townsville. Brother Kim tried to assure him that all was OK while everyone suspected the worst. Joe replied, "Bullshit, Kim!" "The sweetest words he could have heard, said Kim."

From Bora they expanded to Cathedral Station, north west of Winton, north Queensland. During the 1997 Wik debate, I recall flying in to see them. John had brought out the tractor to clear a makeshift airstrip. The boys were mustering. It was excruciatingly hot. Norah showed us her latest paintings ("All my siblings and I are artistic in some way."), prepared lunch for all, and showed us over the property. Pastoralists sympathetic to Aboriginal native title holders and committed to racial equality but with no romantic notions about land rights and reconciliation, they wanted to talk about what all this legal and political talk out of Canberra would mean on the ground. They insisted on refuelling our plane, wishing us well. As Norah says, "Grazier's life is a constant gamble, an educated gamble…Sometimes I felt I was carrying the drought on my own, watching the stock."

Norah's whisperings in the grass have always come from the land, her family and her God – each child a gem, the grandchildren sparkling in their variety. When her little grandson Tyler died five days after being hit by a car, the family took him to his final resting place on the back of a Landrover with everyone aboard. Her son Matt's electrocution is the epilogue of her book and the nightmare of her life. Two nights after the funeral, the 'Wet' starts. "Crashing thunder tearing the humid stillness". Being neither mad, mercenary nor missionary, Norah Kersh has endured drought and flood as child and mother. Readers from the outback will need only change the property names and imagine different roads; city folk will be introduced to a new world – the outback of old Australia where faith is sure and simple, the weather always in doubt, and the risks of survival enlarged through the prism of distance.

Fr Frank Brennan SJ AO

Joe's first lesson on a bike was given by Matt at the Cathedral station shearing shed. With the purchase of Cathedral we had inherited a Honda 200XR. The bike was reasonably powerful and quite big for Joe's nine year old frame.

"Here Joe. Hop on and I'll sit behind".

Joe's legs were able to reach the ground only one at a time, and then with the bike on a dangerous slant.

"Now," instructed Matt, "You need to give it a bit of acceleration when you kick it into gear".

Joe did as he was told, his small hand clamped on the accelerator. With a roar the bike rocketed out from under Matt. Joe clung for dear life, front wheel in the air, back tyre spitting out gravel. Exhaust fumes filled the air as the bike came to rest, climbing the rails of the count-out yard.

With the seat of his jeans ripped, and a sprained wrist, Matt reckoned "We'll give it another go tomorrow. Ay, Joe?"

That, though, came much later. First, I'll track back.

Splashed with Sunlight

Tolstoy in *Anna Karenin* begins with "All happy families are alike but an unhappy family is unhappy in its own fashion." My childhood was of the former variety. Born the third youngest in a family of eleven children, ten girls and one boy, there is no doubt that I was spoilt with attention. The little ones in our large family had only to utter a cry before several older siblings were there to do our bidding.

My parents, Ned O'Brien and Norma Perrottet, were married in 1924. Claire was their first child, born in 1925, then followed Patricia, Nan, Elizabeth, Maureen, Bernadette, Philomena, and Frances. I was born 22 June 1941 (the day the Russians came into the war); our brother Miceal was born in 1943. Eight years later our baby sister, Monica, came along in our mother's forty-seventh year – a surprise and delight. Monica was the age of some of her nieces and nephews, so inhabited a different world from her older siblings.

We grew up on Yahgunyah, a sheep property fifty miles north of Warren in western New South Wales on the black soil plains noted for merino wool-growing sheep. Yahgunyah had a beautiful old homestead, built in at least three stages, the oldest part dating back to the 1800's. The kitchen, laundry, and breakfast room were constructed of hand-adzed slabs. Ornate patterns of curlicues and flowers, hand-painted in many colours decorated the pressed tin walls and ceiling of the dining room. Looking at these I imagined all sorts of creatures in the designs. Wide verandahs surrounded the main part of the house. Here we roller-skated, rode bikes and even practised hitting a tennis ball.

I would open my eyes on a frosty morning, tumble eagerly from beneath grey blankets and into some clothes. From sleepout onto the verandah and like a dart, I would head for the warmth of the kitchen at the other end of the house. "Dad'll be up", I'm thinking. Indeed he is, having brought wood from the wood-heap near the chook yard. Clean scent of yarran smoke wafts through the air, as Dad now lifts the kettle on the stove and shakes a handful of tea-leaves into the enamel teapot.

"Good morning. You're up bright and early. How about a cup of tea?" Pink cheeked with pleasure I get out a cup. As small children we were not permitted to drink tea, except at this time when we were offered a cup and felt grown up sitting in the kitchen having an early morning cup with Dad.

The house was situated beside a large dam on the Back Creek, a tributary of the Merri Merri. Making good use of it in summertime we all learned to swim early. In dry times we had to be careful not to waste water. It was pumped by the windmill on the bank into an overhead tank, then on to the house. A number of large corrugated iron tanks caught rain water off both the house and hayshed. In the garden were citrus trees - orange, mandarin, and lemon. Purple bougainvillea splashed lavishly over the trellis. Over the years our mother established a rose garden, along with many shrubs, and year by year beds of stocks, zinnias, delphiniums, freesias by the hundred - each tree and flower tended with loving care. She cherished them the more, I feel, because of the scarcity of water. Many a summer evening we had our meal on the lawn as Dad told us the names of the constellations, the Southern Cross swinging its course overhead.

I am ever grateful to my parents. They did not believe the axiom "children should be seen and not heard". Instead we were encouraged to have opinions and ask questions. In our high ceilinged sitting room, with its fireplace flanked by bookshelves, was a large cabinet wireless. Dad, whilst listening to the news, often jotted down notes – then at meal times, out from his flannel shirt pocket would come the Cooper's note book and he would tell us of world events, asking us questions, inviting discussion. Conversation was never dull. The piano too, was in the sitting room, music sheets stacked on top. Strains of *Remembrance* and the *Norwegian Cradle Song* floated along the verandah as Mum played in the evening.

Sometimes people tried to sympathise with my father having "all those girls". He stoutly maintained we were just as good as boys. We were expected to saddle our own horses, muster the stock and help with the yardwork. As we grew older Dad gave Mike or me a turn on the drafting gate at the end of the narrow drafting race, whipping the gate back and forth, sending the ewes this way, the wethers that. All the while watching closely the ear marks to distinguish sex or age, cursing heartily as a bunch of lambs rushed through the wrong way, or "You dopey coot!" at a ewe that had outsmarted me, skinning my knuckles as the gate slammed against the side of the race. Counting sheep or cattle is an art. When we were little Dad used to get us to keep tally for him as he called out "One hundred. Two. Three" as sheep poured through the gate. We picked up a stick for each hundred. Dad counted by threes, so when he reached 33 added 1 to make the hundred. This method allowed for quick counting as animals baulked, or bunched and rushed past. We were encouraged to count too. "Don't give up if you lose count,"our Dad instructed "Just guess and keep going". This worked pretty well when we compared counts at the end. I still only count by twos though - the thirty three plus one defeated me. My sisters and I were not asked to do heavy "men's work" for example, killing sheep - thank goodness. Dad would patiently show us, while fencing, how to tie a figure 8 knot in 10-gauge wire, or how to use the wire strainer without having it slip off the wire and hit us.

Long before we heard the word *conservation,* my father demonstrated it. He loved the country and taught us how even the smallest creature or plant had its place in the scheme of things. He would stop to point out some miracle of nature, appreciating each facet of creation. Digging around the cabbages in the vegetable garden he called me over to see the transparent pink earthworms in the damp earth. "Yuk!" I stared fascinated. "These little fellers are very good for the garden; they dig through the soil and let the air in."

My older sisters were taught in the school room separate from the house. A teacher lived with the family. Our O'Brien cousins from Mayfield, just three miles away, and the Loudon children from Noonbah came across on horses or in a sulky. When the older ones began boarding school, the numbers were too few for this subsidized school, so Mum taught the younger members of the family by correspondence. Lessons came on the mail from Blackfriars Correspondence School in Sydney. Writing lessons began with us labouring over lines of pothooks. Our early readers were full of heroic stories. A coloured picture sticks in my mind: A girl in a boat straining against the mighty ocean storm, her red hair streaming out in the wind, as she rows valiently onwards to rescue people in a shipwreck - the story of Grace Darling. Do kids of today have such stouthearted heroes to inspire? There were weather charts to fill in, recording temperature, rainfall and cloud formation: Cumulus? Cirrus? Nimbus?

The wonderful monthly school magazine brought the next instalment of an exciting serial, stories and poetry. We were introduced to Blake's 'The Tiger':

Tiger, tiger burning bright,
In the forest of the night,
What immortal hand or eye,
Could frame thy fearful symmetry?'

and Henry Kendall's 'Song of the Cattle Hunters':

As the beat and the beat
Of our swift horse's feet
Start the echoes away from their caves.

Here and there, Bernadette and Philomena had a hand in supervising our lessons. I think my language improved remarkably when Bernie helped me with composition. At about age eight I had to describe a sunset. Bernie, with a better command of English had suggested a couple of phrases: *Aweful splendour* and *gilt edged clouds.* The return mail brought the teacher's comment: "Was this all your own work, dear?" Mum took pains trying to get me to spend more time finishing my work. Near enough was good enough for me. I was forever painting and drawing. "Do you think a little more shadow here?" my mother would tactfully ask, or "Perhaps go over those edges to tidy it up". It took forty years or more for me to appreciate what she was trying to get through to me. Then, with daughters of my own, I delighted in making their dresses and pinnies, frills around the hem and crochet edges. It took me back to Mum's hand work which was impeccable.

Making our dresses, often embellished with fine smocking, hems and buttonholes were always beautifully hand stitched. Baby clothes were smocked and embroidered on fine cotton, linen or wool. Never synthetic!

We were encouraged to read so long as it was in siesta time; no lazing around with a book when there was work to be done! Around the fire on a winter night we laughed over the antics of Wodehouse's Jeeves. Dad would take down a beautifully bound Popular Encyclopedia (being Dictionary of Science and Arts, Literature, Biography, History and General Information). Lying on the floor with one of these tomes we children were facinated with engravings, maps and all kind of wonders. I read *He Went with Vasco de Gama* and *He Went with Marco Polo*. In the office at Yahgunyah there were bookshelves up to the ceiling, and ever a scattering of half-read books lying around where my sisters had put them down. *Norah of Billabong* by Mary Grant Bruce was given me for one of my birthdays. I loved the story of the colonial family, complete with Chinese cook, whose adventures took them through the goldrush days, war, growing up and falling in love. I couldn't wait for Christmas to be given the next in the series.

Childhood was full of sunshine. Playing across the creek with my brother and sisters on swings and a hammock slung between gum trees provided endless enjoyment. Bushies and Bobbies was a favourite game, with cousins (more children) around the woolshed with numerous yards, woolroom, engine room, benches and spaces to hide. Even better, and a bit scary, <u>under</u> the shed, with spider webs hanging in dark corners, we would crouch hiding, dust particles dancing in sunlit strips which filtered through slatted sheep pens.

Behind the garage we made cubby houses from the wooden boxes our groceries came in, always a work in progress. Sheets of tin and wheat bags were used in creative ways "I bags that bit of ashes, to make the icing" I would cry, as my sister, with a stick, industriously mixed her chocolate mud cake in a tin. We played Countries: Every player took the name of a country then stood in a circle around the player with the ball. He or she would hurl the ball as far as possible calling the name of one country. "China!" Everyone would run, except China, who would race to retrieve the ball and yell "Stop!" China would try to hit the country closest to him with the ball, and the game progessed as that child was "in". Happy days indeed.

Golden Fleece

In 1950 wool prices boomed, allowing my parents to pay off the property they had purchased in the 1920's. Record floods in 1950 and again in the mid-fifties drowned or bogged a good many sheep. Collecting "dead wool" was one of our occupations. A lump of wool in the distance indicated a dead sheep, however it needed to be dead long enough and dried out, to allow us to gather and shake the dust and bones from the parchment-like carcase. Sounds dreadful and I admit, smelly. It was a commonplace practice then, and worth taking to the shed to be baled and sold as dead wool.

During one of the floods we were all helping move a mob of sheep to higher ground in the Mail Box paddock. The creek had risen and risen and was spreading, as ankle deep in cold water and mud we pushed reluctant sheep towards higher ground. I noticed my sister, Philomena, struggling to get an old ewe moving, and then, as old ewes do, she gave up and lay down. There was Phil, on this bitterly cold day, taking off her own woolen cardigan and draping it over the old sheep. Ages later, riding along in lovely grass mustering this same paddock, I came across a little pile of white bones draped with fragments of Philomena's brown woolen cardigan.

This decade brought a plague of rabbits. Rabbits in the thousands, eating everything in their path. On a hot day scores of them could be seen squatting in the shade of tree or roly poly.

Landholders spent a big percentage of their time combatting this pest. Dad bought his first tractor, a red David Brown, to plough out rabbit warrens which riddled the lighter country. Mike and I used our treasured pocket knives to skin the rabbits we had trapped, then stretch the skins over bowed wire to dry out. We felt like millionaires when Dad sold a wheat bag full for thirty shillings.

Picture an army disposal Chevrolet as it drives slowly across a drought parched paddock. On the back, cotton shirts flapping, bare legs dangling, we children are clutching wheat bags with grain trickling out over the side. Hundreds of hungry sheep come running amidst clouds of dust, to stop and drop their heads as soon as they reach the yellow trails. Drought! Did it worry us? Not a bit of it. It was all fun.

Our parents never put their worries on to us. They must have had a few. Living a good distance from town, rearing a large family through the depression years, short of everything, followed by the war years with rationing of food, clothing, and especially of petrol, must not have been easy. My mother told me that before my time, through the 1930's, swaggies who came along were always given some work, food and sometimes boots to go on with. It didn't matter that there was not an abundance lying around.

Somewhere in our family archives a shadowy photo shows a fully loaded wagon of wool behind a team of camels. This photo was taken at Yanda on the Darling River, where my father was before his brother, Jim, and he bought Yahgunyah in 1924, and later the adjoining Mayfield. Indian and Afghan camel men with their strings of camels were the backbone of inland transport from early days. They reached the furthest outposts of the dry interior, laden with goods of all description.

The beginning of the end for these pioneers came with the Second World War. Surplus army vehicles and four-wheel drives took over, casting the faithful camel into obsolescence. Only today are camels making a comeback. Wild camels are being mustered from the rugged hills around Cloncurry and sandhills of the Territory to be used to mitigate the spread of imported prickly bush. Camel racing at Alice Springs and Boulia in the Desert Sands Races, and at other townships is becoming increasingly popular. Ironically Australia's isolated conditions have evolved a remarkably healthy animal which is now exported back to the Middle East.

As a small girl I recall the sound of horsebells:- Umber Din's horses, content in our horse paddock. Umber Din's visit, perhaps once a year, was an exciting event. His horsedrawn caravan stopped at each property, opening up to display drawers and shelves overflowing with laces and cloths. We children would gather round the tailboard of the wagon to peer into the depths of the mysteries within. In my fancy I see Umber Din at twilight alongside his caravan, hunched on a three legged stool, a long curved tube pipe reaching into a bowl on the ground (opium perhaps?), horsebells intermittently sounding their comforting tune. Little did I know that years later that nostalgic sound would become part of my life across the continent.

The sprawling weatherboard and corrugated iron shearing shed came to life in June with the arrival, in an assortment of vehicles, of the shearing team. The steam engine with its towering fly wheel was fired up to power the overhead gear. Red coals in the fire box reflected on the brass whistle which was sounded at knock off time. The thump, thump of the engine and slap of leather belt on pulley wheel accompanied the buzz of the combs and cutters. Fleeces peeled off as sweating shearers worked for a high tally, good natured banter passing between them. "Tar boy!" a shout from the shearer at the far end of the board. Rousie drops his broom and snatches up blackened tar pot to dab the fly-blown backside of the new shorn sheep, before its shearer shoves it down the chute to the countout pen. "You'll make a shearer one day mate," to the sweating roustabout.

Roustabouts ran along the board swooping on the new shorn fleece, then back to the wool table expertly flinging it fan-shaped onto the wooden table. Classer and wool-roller then sorted and classed before piling it into the overflowing wool bins. The wool presser was always working into smoko* time, wielding the long handle of the Koertz wool-press. The whole sepia-toned, lanoline scented scene comes back to me.

As days passed, bales mounted up, stacked two and three high. We children played hide and seek among them, able to slip down the gaps and disappear. "Give a signal!" the seeker would call, whereupon a muffled hoot could be heard emerging from a crevice between bales. Our guardian angels must have worked overtime as no harm came to us.

This was an exciting time for us children. Before shearing started, sheep had to be mustered to paddocks close to the shearing shed. Each morning during shearing, a couple of us were assigned to carry milk, fresh from the cows, to the shearers' cook. We loved this, as inevitably he would let us sample his cooking: "Here, try these buns for me. See if they are O.K." Shy as we were we didn't need much encouragement as the delicious buns issued from the oven of the huge cast iron stove.

---

* *Morning and afternoon tea*

Bringing sheep up to the yards we liked to time it around smoko time. We would hurriedly hitch our horses to a rail, and join the team in the wool room. There sat the big teapot and trays laden with slabs of sultana cake or fresh cooked buns covered with clean tea towels. A treat awaiting.

*   *   *   *   *

We attended Sunday Mass at Quambone, just twelve miles to the north of Yahgunyah. Quambone Station, surrounded by shady trees, white fence in front, was the first station taken up in that area. Around it had grown a scattering of shearer's houses, a sawmill, the Hotel with a pepper tree, its extensive branches shading the verandah. Across the flat, a corrugated shed where Aboriginal kids played around, sharing an old bike. The baker's shop, store, school, and Bush Nurse's house with gauzed-in verandah sat comfortably by the road. The priest drove out from Coonamble for Mass at Quambone every two weeks.

It was our treat after Mass, while adults talked seasons and other matters, for all the kids to trail round to the store, a shilling or two in hand. "I'm getting licorice allsorts," my cousin might say. "What about you get Fantails and we'll share?" It was a good arrangement. I'd envy the Burtenshaw children whose parents owned the shop, imagining they could have lollies whenever they liked. They were also glamourous in my eyes because those dark haired little girls were good on their ponies on sports days, and their big brothers were rough-riders at the rodeo.

On alternate Sundays we headed in the opposite direction to Mass at Marthaguy, a tin dance-hall on the Marthaguy Creek. The night before, as well as polishing shoes, we packed sandwiches. Arriving at Marthaguy the men lit the fire and put billies on, while children - in best clothes - chased each other along the creek. In the hall, rugs were thrown on the floor for babies to lie on, toddlers crawled round or were handed toys as Mass proceeded. Church was a good experience for me. God was loving and bountiful as far as I was concerned. He came with billy tea at Marthaguy Hall. After Mass sandwiches were laid out on the supper table and hot billies brought forth. In those pre-Vatican II days, we fasted from midnight on Saturday.

Mass at Marthaguy

For forty miles and more they come,
With tell-tale dents and rattles, wreathed in sunburnt battle scars,
Down nameless roads and wrinkled tracks that send the dust sky high,
They head this way, for here today, there's Mass at Marthaguy.

The Perrys, Brennans, Kersh, O'Briens (some seventeen at least),
The seniors send the plate around, the juniors tend the priest,
A mother holds her babe-in-arms and croons a lullaby,
A small child weeps, and Grandpa sleeps, through Mass at Marthaguy.

Then now our Mass is over, the time for all to chat,
A cup of tea, a yarn with friends, a word with Father Pat,
And these kind folk of solid faith are all the reasons why,
They have their Mass but once, alas, each month at Marthaguy.

R.J Stanley

Fairy Floss and Boxing Troupe

Through the 1940's petrol rationing of war years meant that car trips were kept to a minimum. Most people seemed to be in frugal mode until 1950 when wool prices lifted. Even a trip to town was an event, so the Show was an occasion we looked forward to from year to year. Show day couldn't come soon enough. We children were almost exploding with delight as Dad parked the car, nose in towards the arena. Decked out in good clothes, clutching unaccustomed money we set forth; Fran in a new woollen twin set Mum had ordered from David Jones catalogue, me in corduroy jacket. "I still remember the joy of a parcel in the mail," recalls Fran, "the smell of the new garment, tissue wrapped in a cardboard box." First port of call was the children's section in the pavilion where most of us had drawings, poems or compositions carefully mounted on cardboard. Here or there the sought after card decorated with royal blue fronds of wheat: First Prize. By this, having collected a few cousins we would make our way through the sheep stalls where Dad generally had sheep or fleeces on show. Here were rows of pens with well groomed sheep standing in aromatic fresh hay, men in hats deep in discussion leaning on rails draped in prize ribbons. Shouts of triumph from Phil, "Arthur has won champion ewe!" I don't remember how our pet ewe lamb came to be called Arthur, but it stuck with her. Under Philomena's care she grew up without the usual pot belly of the poddy lamb, to gain Champion at Coonamble Show.

These inspections over, we ranged towards the most exciting part of the show, sideshows, merry-go-rounds and dodgem cars. Past stalls spiked with celluloid kewpie dolls in net skirts, twirling celluloid windmills on sticks and balloons fluttering on strings. Show people calling out. They came from a different, far more exotic world, rings in their ears, tattoos and cheeky voices calling us confidently to "Have a go!" Furthermore, they lived in caravans, painted and decorated, and they travelled.

There were carousels, carved horses - black, white and dappled with flaring nostrils moving up and down, up and down until the music of the record wound down and those horses stopped. But Oh! The magic of it! It is with me still.

Pink fairy floss tempted us as we made our way to the Gill Bros. Rodeo tent. The Gill brothers also had sisters. They wore fringed chaps with silver stars sparkling as they rode the buckjumpers round the ring. That was the life, I thought. There was something especially for the kids. A few mild looking donkeys and Shetland ponies were led into the ring. Kids were invited to catch and ride one for eight seconds, with the amazing offer of a five pound prize for the first one to do it. Now! This was something we could do, or so we thought. Children swarmed through the ropes, it would be a cinch. Well! It wasn't long before the kids were falling back through the ropes. Those sweet little animals were feral! When two or three kids managed to corner one kicking, snapping torpedo, and leg up one child on its back, the animal just ducked its head, kicked up its back legs and the rider slid off its fat shiny back. The five pound prize was safe.

Jimmy Sharman's Boxing Troupe drew us like a magnet. On a tall platform across the front of the tent stood a line of fierce looking pugilists in satin shorts and gowns, arms crossed over brawny chests. Jimmy Sharman, inveterate showman, spruiking on his loudspeaker "Roll up, roll up, here's your local man, who's going to take his chance? There's ten pounds to be won. Or Tiger here, three times champion in the Big Smoke". Meanwhile Tiger does a bit of dancing round and throws a few punches in the air. The gathering crowd always included a few who had had a beer or two, encouraging one of their mates to "have a go". Excitement built up as Mr. Sharman invited the encounter. Before long the local lad would be up on the platform in boxing gloves alongside the "professionals". There's a saying which goes something like this "A bloke on the booze is no match for a half baked professional". We children were fascinated with the whole spectacle. Our mother, of course, completely disapproved of our interest in this field.

Sharmans travelled the country for years. Jimmy Sharman refereed the fights and was well known for his care and fairness.If indeed, as sometimes happened, he did pick up real local talent they often went on to Sydney Stadium and a boxing career.

Open Doors

Yahgunyah, our childhood home, was open to many visitors: Sheep buyers, stock and station agents, the children of city friends, missionary nuns and priests from far-off places. Also, over the years, blind boys from interstate Queensland and the Northern Territory, and one boy from Vietnam, who attended St. Edmund's School for the Blind in Sydney, came to Yahgunyah for school holidays. These boys leapt into station life with enthusiasm, joining in whatever was taking place. Though they couldn't see they could distinguish by sound e.g. which neighbor's vehicle was coming along the road. They would run rings around us playing chess. Black pieces were identified from white by a small point on top though otherwise shaped exactly as castle, knight or pawn. The chess board had raised squares. Several of the boys played the guitar. David Kerin was from Tennant Creek, a solid brown skinned little boy when we first got to know him. He had a great sense of humour. Strumming his guitar he sang Slim Dusty songs as he sat on the verandah after tea on the lawn on summer nights. Subsequently, David trained to be a physiotherapist, I think the first Aborigine to train in that field, and became well known in sporting circles as a sports therapist. Mum learned to make Braille books, painstakingly pressing the symbols into the thick paper. Later she got a Braille typewriter, making the operation slightly more high tech.

"I wish you wouldn't ride that horse, dear," was an oft repeated refrain. Mother worried for us. Dad wouldn't allow us to race our horses home from the Ridge Paddock gate; it would get them into the habit of wanting to take off as soon as the gate was closed. In spite of that, our spirited horses usually began to dance and crow-hop at that last gate. Anxious, Mum may have been, however she could be relied upon to be calm during a crisis, knowing just what to do. On one occasion Monica, my little sister, had come off her horse; after catching her foot in the stirrup she was dragged upside down till her boot came off. Mercifully, beyond a fright and scratches, she wasn't hurt. My mother gathered Monica up as my horse pounded up. "Just go to the bathroom dear," I was instructed "and get the mercurochrome from the second shelf". She settled Monica on a chair. "I'll bathe this cut with warm water, and soon you will be as good as new". Monica lapped up the attention and made the most of being an invalid.

When I was three or four years old I was given a surprise. My mother was going on an infrequent trip to Sydney. The family stood around the car saying goodbye. I was crying, not wanting her to go, or wanting to go with her. As she hugged me goodbye she whispered, "Run up to my room, when I've gone. There's something on the bed for you". Mystified, I ran around the verandah as soon as the car drove off, and through the gauze door into Mum's and Dad's room. Lying on the white pillows was a big rag doll. I could hardly believe my eyes. "Penelope" I called her. She had a round face with painted brown eyes and pink cheeks, a couple of brown curls escaped from under her stitched on bonnet. Her dress was made from apricot coloured material. My tears were over. It wasn't my birthday or Christmas! A present out of the blue from Mum. How I loved that doll!

Boarding School
Brigidine Convent, Coonamble

My carefree life came to an end, when at age twelve I was taken to boarding school in Coonamble, thirty-five miles away. Mum and Dad drove to town to deposit me at the convent. After interviewing the formidable Mother Dominic in the convent parlour my parents kissed me good-bye and left. The thought of being within boundaries! The long weeks, stretching ahead without seeing family and home, seemed like an eternity. I was bereft. (The same feeling was mirrored in me years later when John and I took our elder daughter, Rosana, to boarding school in Brisbane. I felt I was abandoning our precious daughter.)

In navy serge tunic, crisp blouse and a tie, I felt like an alien. It was traumatic to be among a lot of nuns who all looked alike and with children I had never seen before. Added to this, was all I had to remember: A bell to wake up, a bell for meals, a plethora of rules. It was frightening. Would I ever get the hang of it? My older sisters Philomena and Fran had gone on to Loreto in Sydney, so I never had a sister with me at boarding school. I missed them bitterly.

School in a classroom with assorted boys and girls was a new experience. When assigned our homework at the end of the first day I made the mistake of asking what homework was. The children all laughed. I hadn't heard the term "homework". It didn't make sense to me who was definitely not "at home". I was utterly embarrassed.

Days were run to a timetable. I think schools were organized along rather military lines. After the war authority and discipline were next to godliness, so we stood in lines, kept silence till we were told we may speak, and polished our leather lace-up shoes till we could see our faces in them. This is just the way society was; it didn't do much for homeliness and homesick bush kids. Considering the nuns cared for us round the clock, cooked for us and taught us, they did an amazing job. Coaching the boys, Sister Helen would hitch up her long black habit, tuck back her veil and give the boys the rounds of the football field. Mother Vianney, a highly trained musician, taught the up and coming musical talent of Coonamble. As well as teaching piano and violin she taught us singing. We regularly stood on our forms as she or one of the talented Bacigalupo pupils conducted. St. Patrick's Day concert was a big occasion when everyone, from the infants' class up, performed. Year by year much preparation went into making backdrops and costumes – and year by year Coonamble turned out for the big night.

In 1883 the first Irish Brigidines had come straight from their homeland to what must have been a dry, dusty little town. Their passage out was on the *Chimbarazo* on which, coincidentally, my grandfather was sailing. All were from County Carlow.

The convent was a beautiful two-storied weatherboard building. The upstairs dormitory overlooked a wide bend of the Castlereagh River. The 1950's brought a series of floods to what was usually a dry sandy expanse of riverbed. Big rains in the Warrumbungles, east of Coonamble, quickly filled tributaries to come racing down the slopes into the main stream cutting across the plains. The Castlereagh is the fastest flowing inland river in NSW. From our dormitory windows we boarders gazed in fascination at the brown waters of the flood swirling by.

Each week during summertime we walked along the bank beneath the overhanging river gums and across the bridge for a swim in the town pool. There were no safety fences but we all had a sensible respect for the Castlereagh in flood. During the flood it was exciting watching from the safety of the bridge, despite shuddering from the impact of rushing water. Debris and old logs went tumbling by, being dragged under in frothing whirlpools, then spearing out to be carried who knows where?

My parents' trips to town were rare enough. Dad always came with a sheep to go in the convent larder. What joy when I got a message that they were in town, and I could go out to lunch! For this I had to don hat and gloves and be inspected by Sister's unerring eye before seeing my parents. Pity help if some busybody around town reported a boarder who dared take the hat off, or walked along the street eating an ice cream. Ladies did not do that! We would dine at one of the Greek cafes, either the Monterey or the Busy Bee, and eat a mixed grill of fried sausage and egg with some beetroot and lettuce - a total gourmet delight.

Phone calls were received only when necessary. If we were summoned to the parlour for a call from home, the sound of my parent's voice over the crackly party line brought forth a shower of tears. Poor Mum! I guess she was left to worry as her child placed the receiver down and ran off to forget the emotion in a game of tennis.

Loreto

I was sent to Loreto at Normanhurst to finish my schooling. Sydney was even further from home. It is disgraceful how unappreciative I was of the opportunity given me by my parents. A beautiful school set in large grounds backing onto bushland where we went for walks, two by two along a bridle track. Near a rocky creek an overhanging rock formed a sort of cave; it was reputed a hermit lived here. I never saw the hermit, but his abode lent fascination to the surrounding bushland. Loreto had excellent teachers including the forward thinking art teacher, Mother Evangeline, and dear old Mother Perpetua, who could remember every boarder back to the year dot.

"Homesick" we called it. Longing for the spaciousness of home I would imagine myself mustering the Long Plain Paddock, wind whipping through my hair, fragrant tang of dry grass brushing beneath my horse's hooves – as I gazed through the plate-glass windows of my classroom overlooking trimmed lawns and trees softly green, through a mist of rain. Confined. So homesick! A fellow boarder from a farm at Gular and I were wallowing in the condition. We decided the best thing would be to just get on a train and go home. We thought our parents would see that we really didn't need to be cooped up in boarding school…simple as that. We asked a day-pupil to purchase tickets for the Western Mail, as the train was called. Luckily this pupil had more common sense than we adventurers, and let one of the nuns know. Our plot discovered, we were hauled before the head nun. We felt the keen interest of the other children at our summons to the office. Even now, fifty-something years later, my cheeks practically burn with mortification at the thoughtlessness of my 15-year old self. Needless to say my parents were less than impressed. My sister Bernie was returning to Australia with her husband Michael. They had married in Ireland, Michael's homeland. Mum and Dad were coming to Sydney to meet them, a family celebration. I felt ashamed that my escapade had to be discussed as they were summonsed to the principal's office. I simply couldn't give any good reasons for my behavior other than overwhelming homesickness. My throat clenched up in misery, unable to express my feelings to my parents.

Perhaps there is an upside. I have a real fellow feeling for seemingly sophisticated young people who do foolish things on impulse, with little thought for the consequences.

I guess I absorbed a little education, but my focus was on holidays and freedom. What young horses were waiting to be handled? What was my brother Mike up to? The boys seemed to have much more fun at Red Bend College in Forbes. They were allowed to swim in the Lachlan River and swing from branches to go flying into the river. Mike claims he did his share grubbing out the big old gums where the football field was being built for the new college. Creative thinking by the teachers when handing out detention!

Subsequently Red Bend became co-educational. A generation later several of my nieces and nephews attended the college.

A family tragedy occurred during the Christmas holidays. It was Boxing Day at Yahgunyah. Family and friends had gathered for a picnic across the creek. Our six-year old niece, Claire - Nan and John Waterford's daughter, was drowned. People were splashing around having fun, some of the children trying out newly acquired presents of blow-up floaters. I was towelling down dripping, crying, Marianne. "Claire's under the water," she said. I dropped the towel and rushing out saw my sister Maureen, in sundress, carrying a tray of glasses. "Claire's gone under the water!" I repeated stupidly. Somehow Claire had drifted to a deep place and gone under. The alarm went up, agonizing minutes dragged by as we searched; then her Uncle Bill Crawford carried her out of the water. It was too late. It seemed unbelievable such a vital little girl was lost to us. Desperate for her parents and their little family, I still have frightening dreams involving water in all shapes and forms. My children think I'm paranoid about water safety. Such an experience is never forgotten.

Coming Home

Loreto girls wept as they made their farewells to school days. I'm not proud of it but my main feeling was one of relief – just to be going home at last. I think now I was prejudiced before I even arrived at Loreto. One of the nuns at Coonamble had asked me rather sternly "Is Coonamble not good enough?" A farm girl from Ireland, I think she saw me as a privileged grazier's daughter (and I was, in many ways). Never mind, I owned only one pair of shoes and my parents had always worked hard to make ends meet, let alone going without to send their four youngest daughters to complete school in Sydney. This one remark cut me to the heart, it seemed so unfair. I didn't want to go anywhere!

There was one attraction though. My cousin Dominica, a student at Loreto, had told me that periodically they had films, or "pictures" as we called them. This seemed magical to me, in the days when a television was a picture in a geographical magazine. The first film I ever saw was in the open air picture theatre in Warren. Sitting in a row of canvas chairs with my family I was rapt in the story of *The Overlanders* with Chips Rafferty the star. There was a little girl called Margaret with blond plaits, on the droving trip. That night I was introduced to something beyond my imagination. My next experience was to see *Bush Christmas* in Coonamble. Going to town was exciting enough, as darkness descended driving towards town, suddenly a sprinkling of lights strung across the flat horizon, my first sight of a town at night seemed like fairyland.

Unfortunately, at boarding school periodic movies barely made up for my misery. I felt a foreigner and my attitude did nothing to help. Why did I not grasp the opportunity presented?

I had a few friends, but I didn't really connect with many girls at school. I didn't analyse it at the time, but looking back I guess I didn't need a best friend. My family at home comprised my best friends and I couldn't wait to get home to where I felt I belonged. Could it be one of the perils of the large family? Being sufficient unto itself? My parents example of being "other centred" has gradually worked into my consciousness.

Old fashioned it seems today, but it was fairly normal then for country girls to go home for a time after leaving school. So, with no thoughts of university and exciting career, I was happy to be working around the house and happier still out working stock. A prevailing idea, especially among Catholics (I blush to admit) that women didn't need to go on to higher education, was also part of my parents' thinking – even though on most subjects they were liberal minded. My sisters had gained entry to university but were not encouraged in this. One academic of the day wrote an article in the Sydney Morning Herald entitled *Don't put your Daughters on the Campus*. This was in the 1950's. Appalling it looks today but maybe judging yesterday with today's eyes is misleading too.

By the time I left school, my sister Claire had entered the Marist Missionary Sisters, to spend many years in the Solomon Islands as teacher, artist and writer. Patricia was married to Bill Waterford and living in the fabulous opal fields of Lightning Ridge. Nan, Elizabeth, and Maureen were married, Bernadette was on a working holiday in England. Philomena was a governess to nephews at Lightning Ridge, and Fran was doing a business course preparing to travel overseas with friends.

Phil and Fran were always making things. If not cakes, it was clothes. If races or a ball was on the calendar, there were swathes of waterwave taffeta, organza or some gorgeous material spread out on the sitting room floor with paper patterns being placed this way and that to make the most of the yards of fabric. Fran was the first in the district to wear a "sack" – purple, a very "out there" fashion. In it with her glossy dark hair she looked stunning. She bequeathed this dress to me when she joined the Rosary Sisters, a congregation founded in Tasmania to teach isolated children and support their parents.

Clothes did not hold my interest. Elastic-side boots, coloured shirt and jeans were my favourites. Teen fashion hardly existed. Girls substituted their little girl dresses for boring twin sets and skirts just as suitable for their mothers' age group. Then, sometime in the sixties, the Flower People burst on the scene. I loved the black stockings and flower-in-the-hair look. Bridget Bardot with sultry eyes and tousled hair wearing check gingham and broderie anglais was just 'IT'. I was hooked. Patricia brought me two such dresses from Sydney; I wore them almost to tatters.

A polocrosse club was formed in Quambone. I considered it had all the ingredients a game should have. We had no horse float so I used to ride with my cousin Dominica to meet Eb Hayden at the main road and then on to Gerwa half way. There the Smiths and our horses were loaded, to proceed to Quambone for the day's play. Coming home the exercise was reversed, unloading and riding home in the moonlight. I rode one of our stock horses, Nimbus, for polocrosse. After doing stock work I'd get my racquet and hit the ball round the flat for practice, whenever I had a chance. We travelled locally to compete with other teams; the most memorable trip was to Bourke, when rain (in that country where it rarely rains) brought the competition to an end. It was too dangerous to play on slippery ground. However the social side of our trip didn't suffer.

Our family had grown up on stories of Bourke. Between 1917 and 1924 Dad, with elder brother Jim as manager, had lived on Yanda Station, downriver from Bourke. It was when wool was transported on the river steamers. The split bridge across the Darling at North Bourke remains a reminder of the riverboat era. Even then it was at the whim of weather, with its droughts and floods deciding if the boats could navigate that far.

Yanda extended 45 miles front to back. Yahgunyah hut, an outstation, was twenty-four miles from the station homestead. As the drought worsened stockhorses too poor to work were turned out, to be replaced by pushbikes. When we were children Dad recounted the tale of a man getting lost. This chap was new to the place. He had taken a mob of sheep from Yahgunyah hut to a further out paddock. The job completed, he turned his bike to head back and, ignoring advice thought he would take a short cut. He climbed a fence and made off through the scrub. It was the height of summer, a scorching sun making him light headed. Soon he abandoned his empty waterbag. Meanwhile Dad had come to Yahgunyah hut to pick him up. No Jim (for that was his name). Dad set off, following Jim's tracks. Seeing what had happened he searched, scanning the dry dirt for tracks. They were wandering everywhere. Gnarled mulga branches, black against the afterglow of sunset gave no secrets away. Dad camped, remembering that in a featureless landscape, a person often walks towards anything that is different. Just on daylight he found Jim, almost perished, on the bank of a dry tank. He had thrown away his boots and most of his clothes. It was Christmas morning.

Spellbound we listened to Dad, and learned the lesson: "If you ever get lost, don't get through a fence. Just stay on it and follow it till you come to a gate and a track".

At Yanda when the drought broke about 1922, Dad bought a mob of 5000 sheep at Darr River Downs near Longreach in Queensland. They averaged seven miles a day on the six month droving trip south to Yanda. Droving with Dad were Jack Perrottet (Mum's brother), Jim Alderdice, the man who had been lost, and others. One of Dad's stories from that time concerned an unhappy cook who left a freshly baked damper beside the dinner campfire with a note "I can't cook. Goodbye". He had hailed the train, as the railway line ran beside the route, and went on his way.

Polocrosse in Quambone came to an end with the onset of drought in about 1960. However it restarted many years later when Quambone became a team to be reckoned with.

With cousins and young people along the Marthaguy we had an active social life. Plenty of young people, with jackeroos on most properties. Tennis courts had been built at Marthaguy; we organized matches with Carinda, Quambone, Myall Ridge and Nedgera all in a radius of a hundred miles or so. Tennis clubs had just tennis courts and tin shelter sheds in a paddock.

Bachelor and Spinster balls in my youth were more sedate affairs than those of today. Formal printed invitations were sent to guests – vetted by our parents; usually these guests came from far and wide for the weekend. We often travelled together with our neighbours to the ball. The mix of drink, a good band, young people and popular dances of the day hasn't changed so much. Today, swags are stacked on the back of utes for celebrations to continue into next day. This practice was definitely "not on" for my generation. After the ball, milling out the doors into freezing winter air, we would rush for woollen coats, girls discarding flimsy fancy sandals for warm socks and shoes, to make our way home in non-air conditioned cars. We would arrive home as day was breaking, revealing frost-encrusted grass. Following sleep we shared a family brunch, perhaps played a game of tennis before our friends set off home.

It seemed natural when my older sisters married that they came home for Christmas with husbands and babies. Although when my sister Philomena announced her engagement to Jim Simmons I was happy for her happiness, for the first time I became aware that our family would not always remain the same. She would be missed at Yahgunyah. I was devastated - realizing change was a painful part of growing up. As small children, getting the milking cows in each afternoon to pen up the calves, Phil told me stories. She was, and is, a great reader. The classic *Robbery Under Arms* was related to me as the cows wended their way across the paddock. The romance and excitement as the Marsden brothers drove stolen cattle to the hidden hollow and were beguiled into the bushranging life enthralled me and took me into another realm. When I was old enough to read the book I was not disappointed.

Jackaroo

It is hard not to fall in love at seventeen, sprawling on the lawn on a summer evening. Purple bogainvillea flowering over the verandah roof, a million stars bejewelling the heavens, in the distance a chorus of frogs echoing along the creek. And Jim, playing his mouth-organ. I was entranced by this lovely young man, when fate stepped in.

It was a routine sort of day – the day I met John. Two new jackaroos had arrived at Mayfield. My cousins and I had speculated on what they would be like. Ned had asked for a hand for the day, so one of the jackaroos was coming to help. Dad walked into the kitchen with John as I stirred something on the stove. Here was the new jackaroo, confident, brown hair, college-cut, tanned arms, faded moleskins. "What a gorgeous fella!" was my immediate reaction. Ridiculously shy anyway, I was even more so, as my father introduced us. Having a wooden spoon in my hand gave me something to do at least. I must have stammered a few words before the day's work came to the rescue. There were sheep to draft, lambs to catch and ear-marking pliers to be put into action.

What is it that attracts one to another with such mysterious inevitability? On meeting John, my dreams of Jim were all blown away. I was smitten. This new jackaroo wasn't 'just a pretty face'; he was capable and interesting. At first I thought John's frequent visits to us on weekends were because he and my brother Mike shared an interest in the innards of old cars. John had arrived at Mayfield in a 1927 Chevrolet.

There was to be a twenty-first birthday party for my cousin Dominica, at Mayfield. "Mayf" parties were always fun. In this party my interest was heightened - there were a few new jackeroos in the district, including, John. Interesting indeed. "Would he ask me to dance?" There was no way girls asked boys in those days.

We Yahgunyah kids were quite accustomed to visits to Mayfield. At home in its homey kitchen with its wood stove, enamel canisters arranged on the shelf above - Coffee, Tea, Flour, Rice, and solid table in the middle of the room with one of my cousins, Margaret or Marie, cutting out a batch of scones or bottling fruit on it, like as not.

Dressed up for a party, Mayfield took on new character. Chinese lanterns hung round verandahs, light spilled out on the lawn where our elders gathered. Someone struck up a tune on the piano and as guests took their partners for a dance John walked right to me. Always more comfortable out in a paddock or on a horse behind a mob of sheep, I lacked social assurance. It didn't matter this night. That was not the last dance we had; I danced on air. As months passed, along with dances, tennis parties and gymkanas I discovered we liked each other a lot and seemed to have similar aims and ideals, though I am not sure how much these lofty sentiments entered into our decision that we would marry.

Over the next few years we corresponded as John worked on various places, gaining experience on the land. Practical and keen, he decided this was the life for him.

Our backgrounds were poles apart: John from Pyrmont, the waterfront of Sydney; me from the relatively wide open spaces of western NSW. John was the second-born in a family of four children - Ray, John, Jennice and Margaret. His father, Abe Kersh, came from a Jewish family; his mother Edna was Irish Catholic. John, from the age of about six, lived with his childless aunt and uncle for a number of years. The waterfront was torn with strife during John's youth. His uncle, Ken Lewis, was involved with industrial relations on the wharves and John gained a strong interest in industrial justice. His uncle's heritage was closely linked with the birth of unions in Australia. Ken was one of the children born during the Utopian experiment in Paraguay after the shearers' strike in the 1890's. A group of unhappy shearers and their supporters bought two ships, and with the promise of land in Paraguay set off to form the ideal community. Poet Dame Mary Gilmore, then Miss Cameron, was one of this group. (Years later our children and Mary Gilmore's great grandchildren were on Mt. Isa School of the Air together).

John's father, Abe, was a foreman on the wharves before safety measures of many kinds existed. Men worked in holds of ships with flying wheat dust, or worse, asbestos dust. Like many of the hard working men around him he washed it down with alcohol. John speaks with nostalgia of how Pyrmont children played on the streets when he was small. Safety in numbers, and streetwise enough to know whom to avoid, they got to know the rich tapestry that made up life on the waterfront, where ships from all points of the compass plied their trade.

John's parents saw that their children had a good education and when John completed his final year at Marist Brothers he gained entrance to Duntroon Military College. Before completing the officer training course, John had decided the army life was not for him but had to battle the authorities for permission to leave. He then "shook the dust from his shoes" and headed west as a jackaroo. While still at school John and a mate Rick usually got out of Sydney to spend holidays with friends in the Southern Highlands. The boys had helped their friends to fence on the steep slopes around the Wingercarrabee River, to shoot kangaroos and, mentored by the bachelor brothers, got a taste for bush life. Strangely it was John's friend Rick who later secured a jackaroo's position at my uncle Jim's property, Mayfield. Rick didn't stay, returning to city and insurance office. He mentioned the position on Mayfield to John. Our paths converged.

We were married in the Catholic church in Warren with Monsignior Treacy officiating on Australia Day in 1964.

Gypsies

John and I began married life at Noonbah (which joined Yahgunyah). Old friends and neighbours, the Loudons, were retiring and asked John to manage the place. Noonbah had an additional area on the Macquarie Marshes. I had learned in my correspondence lessons how the explorer Oxley had twice been baffled by these marshes, in his quest for the inland sea. For Oxley, it had once been drought and once floods which foiled his explorations. The Macquarie River breaks up into countless channels spreading over thousands of acres. A mecca for water birds of all kinds, it is also a haunt for wild pigs.

As children we had watched the wavering red glow in the night sky when reeds were burned off at the marshes thirty miles from Yahgunyah.

Now it was our turn, to join with others who had blocks at the marshes, to muster cattle there. The reeds grow thick and higher than a man sitting on a horse. Cattle graze out among the channels making tunnels through the reeds. It was an eerie feeling riding with green walls of reeds surrounding us, horses snorting as they plunged through muddy channels searching to flush out cattle, or sometimes a mob of unfriendly looking razorback pigs. I liked getting back on firm ground.

Within a year we were offered a job at Woodlands near Coonamble, where our first son, Sean, was born. The euphoria of holding my baby was beyond words. Such a beautiful black-haired baby, perfect hands and feet and fingernails, and a little tear on his perfect cheek. My world was complete.

Looking further afield and ambitious for experience, John answered an advertisement in the Country Life, drove up to Queensland for an interview and secured a job as overseer for Ernest Winter on Woolerina, west of Dirranbandi. Woolerina had quite a staff. The homestead, large and modern, had a lovely garden tended by Mrs.Winter and a cowboy gardener.*

A collection of outbuildings, a large workshop, our cottage, men's quarters and horse-yards were scattered around. This was mulga country and drought feeding the order of the day, pushing scrub to keep the stock alive.

In 1966 I was pregnant again, so when the time came I travelled with Sean to Warren to be with my parents. As it happened, Matthew was born the day before my sister's wedding. Fran had spent six years with the Missionary Sisters of Service before deciding her vocation lay elsewhere. The excitement of having another beautiful boy well and truly made up for missing a family wedding. At the hospital Matthew and I were graced with a visit from the wedding party in their finery.

A few days later John, Sean, Matthew and I, with stacks of nappies, were on our way back to the red dirt and mulga of Woolerina. Mum's meat sandwiches packed in a cake-tin in the back, Sean busily organizing his baby brother in his bassinette while I, in some trepidation thought of the long journey.

---

* *Cowboy gardeners were often old stockmen, sometimes disabled by a fall from a horse, who milked the cows and did odd jobs around the homestead.*

John's mind was already ranging to the scrub cutting awaiting in Queensland, drought still a major factor. Leaving Mum and Dad always tugged at my heart-strings, but life was full and there was little time for melancholy.

The rules were strictly laid out about babies, my well-thumbed baby book with instructions on when to expect your baby to sit up, get his first teeth, take the first step and how to wean was religiously followed. Breastfeeding was fine, but when at eight and a half or nine months, weaning time, I was quite nervous about getting it right. Though I had had lots to do with my nieces and nephews as I grew up, and loved every minute with them, a robust two year old seemed so capable and resilient. A small baby was a very different experience – such a great responsibility. I had no one close to ask about these matters. I didn't ring home often. A faint distant voice carried over the miles, on a single wire strung through the scrub, or dipping between flimsy poles marching across treeless plains. It was great to talk to family, but not conducive to long or intimate conversation. Telephone calls were charged for in three-minute segments, the postmistress interrupting with "Three minutes. Are you extending?" So unlike today's scene when communication is almost unlimited and even five-year olds walk around with imaginary telephones clutched between ear and shoulder in imitation of their elders.

Party lines meant we shared the line with three or four neighbours, each with their own ring – e.g. two longs, short long short, two longs and a short (our ring) or three shorts. One got used to one's own particular ring and more or less heard just your own. Maintenance of the line fifty or sixty miles to the nearest post office was shared by neighbours. Trouble with the line usually occurred during the wet, lightning strike splitting a pole or a wild storm leaving the wire caught in branches or touching a fence.

Postmistresses and postmasters running the telephone exchanges were an institution in far flung communities; stories abound of them going the extra mile to be of help. They knew everyone's whereabouts and usually their habits. "You won't get Jo today, she's gone to town". Or "watering the garden at this time, try about sundown". Years later in nor-west Queensland on Christmas Eve we were in town for Midnight Mass. A call was made from Sydney about John's mother being critically ill. Our postmaster, Gordon Rowe, knowing we would not be home rang a friend in town: "The Kersh's would be round at so and so's place after Mass. Could you give them this message?" The message was brought to us. This kind of service was not uncommon.

Bora now has a base tower three hundred feet high with radio digital telephone on which we can hear clearly (except in the wet when it gets temperamental). "Progress" it is called, but strangely we miss the old party line which kept us more in touch.

From Woolerina to Goodooga

There must have been a streak of gipsy in us. Over the years we moved eight times before settling at Bora in north west Queensland in 1979. South of the Queensland border, near Goodooga, John and Nan Waterford and young family lived on the golden Mitchell grass plains at Wombalano. Nan and Pat, my sisters, had married Waterford brothers, John and Bill. Both men were taken prisoners of war in Singapore and were in Changi before being sent to work on the notorious Thai–Burma railway. Now John Waterford was suffering from multiple sclerosis, unable to run the property. The family was to relocate in Sydney. John Kersh offered to go to Wombalano till it was leased or sold.

In spite of drought we had enjoyed our time at Woolerina. Getting to know the itinerant station hands was an education for me who had scarcely left my home district before: Ray, the horse-breaker, who came up with names like *Gravel Rash* - whatever suited the personality of the horse he was training; Tom, who beat me hands down at Chess - we met him years later as a travelling preacher; aboriginal Cam, who still carried a tattered letter written to him by my cousin, for whom he'd worked on Cooinda Station many moons ago; the pregnant 17 year-old with beautiful delicate face, the mechanic's wife. She had never been out of the city before. All these and more. The Hegarty family on Yamma, a neighbouring station, had the priest out for a home Mass occasionally; neighbours partook of the Hegarty hospitality around their generous table on these occasions.

Farewelling all at Woolerina, our worldly goods packed, we set forth. On a dirt road, for they were all dirt roads, windows rolled down for the breeze, we would hit a stretch of bull-dust to be instantly smothered in powdery dust. Fine lawn sheet wrapping Matthew is turned from pastel blue to fawn, along with our eyelashes, faces and clothes. Always a plastic bucket wedged somewhere in the back for wet and smelly nappies – no throwaways then! Matthew was breast fed. When he woke, hungry, I leaned over, lifted him from his bassinet and fed him as the miles rolled by. I was blessed with good-natured babies who took this as a matter of course and went back to sleep.

At Wombalano there was a ill-tempered 32-volt engine which had to be cranked into life in the evening for lights. Its fitful chugging accompanied our family time till lights out.

There was a cast-iron copper outside, to be lit for washing and a wood stove in the kitchen. This was brilliant on a cold winter morning, with the delicious smell of toast cooking on the end of a wire fork.

A faded photo shows a bare shouldered little Sean in overalls wearing his father's boots, in the background the shearing shed. This shed was in the path of a wild wind which tore off half the corrugated iron, rolling it across the landscape into Drysdale-esque shapes. The cyclonic wind cutting a narrow swathe on a hot, still day didn't touch the house from where we watched, only a hundred metres away. Jack Waterford, Nan and John's eldest son, came up for school holidays to help muster for shearing. He was full of originality and ideas then; now he expresses himself as Editor at Large of the Canberra Times.

When Clem Rafferty from Walgett leased Wombalano, we, with the world at our feet, were free to look at options for the future.

The opal town of Lightning Ridge is about fifty miles along the road from Goodooga, across the Narran River past Grawin opal field, and on to the Ridge. Not far from the Ridge lived Pat, Bill and family at Lorne, sheep country studded with opal mines. White mullock heaps of the mines had encroached more and more over their country, rending some paddocks unusable for stock. Pat and Bill had begun to cater for tourists visiting Lightning Ridge. Pat, with her artistic flair, had transformed men's huts and shearers' quarters into attractive accommodation. During the Vietnam War, The Waterfords hosted many servicemen on rest and recreation leave. *

Like opals, the miners were colourful souls, each with his own story - and names like *Russian George; The Hornet*; or the unfortunately-named *Ratter*, and his even more unfortunate wife who was known just as *The Ratter's Wife*. Coming from all parts of the world they lived on the ridge in humpies, built from whatever came to hand. All seemed to find a place at Bill and Pat's table at one time or another. A weathered old character sitting over a cup of tea might casually take a tobacco tin from his pocket, remove the lid to disclose priceless gems - black opal of Lightning Ridge, milky opal from Cooper Pedy or exotic gems from a field in South Africa.

So it was that on a visit to Lightning Ridge we met Dennis O'Leary, an Irishman, in his miner's dwelling of flattened kerosene tins, saplings and bags. A travelled man with the charm of the Irish (in the diplomatic service later). Discussion

---

* *Pat has written about this in her books "Yahgunyah My Gunyah' and 'Intimate Shadows'*

with Dennis ranged far and wide, then came to our long-held idea of doing a couple of years of voluntary work. We had already written to an organization working in Papua New Guinea who had replied "Thanks, but no thanks". They took on as volunteers only trained people such as builders, nurses, teachers. This was understandable. "Why don't you write to Jobst in Broome?" said Dennis. "He's the bishop there, a friend, Bishop for the Kimberley".

That was enough. John composed a letter to Bishop Jobst, outlining his experience, and sent it off to Broome in W.A. A letter came back almost return mail, saying "Yes, come to the west. Father MacGuire is beginning a cattle enterprise at Balgo Mission a hundred and sixty miles south of Halls Creek". We were just the people he needed!

Idealists no doubt. Little did we know this was to be the beginning of seven years of challenge, fun and hardship.

Travelling West

Plans were made for our journey west. We discovered that John Honner (an uncle of my brother-in-law, David) was travelling to La Grange Mission near Broome, to work as a volunteer. We decided to travel in tandem - we in our station wagon, John in his car. What a great travelling companion! He had run his farm near Junee all his life and was a fount of knowledge and wisdom. Our route took us up through Queensland to Mt. Isa, west to the Northern Territory, across to Western Australia, up to the infant town of Kununurra, down to Halls Creek from where John Honner branched west to his destination, while we travelled south the last 160 miles, to Balgo.

Sean was two years old when we made the journey to Balgo in 1967. Matt was six months. North into the sun on mostly dirt roads through Queensland and across the Territory we travelled. Long days; tiring days. Yes, but most of all, exciting! Everything was new to us. With those first impressions of incredibly open plains on the two hundred and thirty miles between Winton and Cloncurry I felt my spirit expand. Between Winton and Cloncurry are Kynuna, a dot on the map, and its few white roofs reflecting the sun, Mckinlay, named after explorer John Mckinlay who went in search of Burke and Wills in 1861. Plains changed to stony Gidyea country scattered with red spires of anthills. Rugged hill country for seventy miles of winding road between Cloncurry and Mount

Isa offering glorious panoramic views. Hues of purple range through to softest pinks and blues.

Along here at Battle Mountain, rest the bones of many Kalkadoon people where they tried to drive white settlers from the area as they trickled in with their livestock. Despite the tribespeople's determination, guns proved superior weapons to the spear. I feel the spirits of the Old people still inhabit that beautiful country.

Throughout most of our journey we camped under the stars, one night gazing at an eclipse of the moon. First, a sliver in shadow till gradually the whole circle, like a copper penny on blue velvet suspended above us. We splashed out on a motel on reaching Mount Isa, enjoying the luxury of a shower and proper wash up. As we fuelled up the vehicle next morning the attendant asked "Where are y'a from. Are y'a coming to stay?"
"No. Just passing through" answered John.
"Good idea" remarked the woman wearily, brushing the hair off her perspiring face.

Leaving Mount Isa, passing low hills and stunted scrub we headed for the border town of Camooweal, one hundred plus miles further along, on the Georgina River. Along the way we regularly passed windmills and cattle troughs, only two cars. Camooweal was home base to drovers who brought cattle from the Kimberley. Across the fateful Murranji Track, with its dry stages and reputation for night rushes of cattle in spooky country, where men were injured as horses galloped in the dark through thick spiky bulwaddi after panicked stock. From Newcastle Waters they crossed the Barkley and the Queensland border, and on to the railhead at Dajarra. *

Many years later our son Brendan was building fences beyond Camooweal.

John looked out for a bit of shade to stop for lunch and a billy of tea. Sometimes a blessed pool of water in a creek gave us an opportunity to give Sean and Matt a cooling swim. I rinsed nappies that dried in the time it took us to have lunch.

From my Diary;

Across The Barkley

Here the plains stretch off into infinity and mirages float about in the distance. Passed Avon Downs shorthorn cattle along creeks, and mobs of horses. Huge piles of black bitumen drums at intervals along the road can be seen for miles. Must be too expensive to cart back or re use. Came into desert country with much spinifex, low bushes - purple wild flowers in places, looks beautiful after a good season. A derelict car on side of road, battered by time with 'Tennant Creek Sudan or bust' scrawled along its side. Looks as if it was 'bust'. Fuelled up at Barry Caves Roadhouse, built of mud. Showers here for two shillings. A sign near the tap: "don't waste the water".

Stopped Dunmara - met Noel Healy and his wife; both entertaining. Noel took up Dunmara forty years ago. Americans have it now. Left north-south road, crossed timbered country with high wiry grass and anthills to Top Springs – pub petrol bowser combined - a lonely place. Left there for Wave Hill 110 miles on, country became open undulating with beautiful feed; crossed lots of creeks, some boggy, all stony. Wave Hill 6158 square miles, arrived there after very slow trip on unformed road just as ringers were trooping in to tea. Huts everywhere, some with spinifex roofs. They employ thirty whites now since unofficial strike by the natives some months ago, over conditions. We were *told here that the track to Halls Creek was completely out. Nine oil trucks had just been through, winching each other over crossings and stewing them up altogether, so we have to go back to Top Springs and around by Kununurra – only about a 500-mile detour! The roads are bad so late this year because of the unusually good wet season. Katherine meat works open 1st May and roads should be graded up. Back to Top Springs, about five men in pub, all with different ideas as to which way we ought get to Halls Creek. Trouble is there is no communication and no traffic. We took the Victoria River Downs track [at own risk] and got through reasonably well. Victoria River is beautiful - very wide. We all washed. Sean and Matt had a ball splashing around.* It must be impressive in full flood. At V.R.D. we were told doubtfully we might get to Timber Creek, as the grader was working on the road. Came through some spectacular hills rising up from flat country, then through Jasper Gorge through which a tropical looking creek runs, cliffs rise up walls on either side - colour is terrific. More wild donkeys. Found Caterpillar driver broken down in middle of creek crossing around which he'd just made a side track. The proper crossing was devastated - huge concrete culverts had washed out and tumbled down creek. Cutaways each end ten feet deep. John H. gave driver lift to Timber Creek where we stayed at pub for night. Creek here is tidal, plenty of crocodiles and good barramundi fishing, they say.*

Further the diary takes us through Kununurra, the mighty Ord River and two hundred and sixty miles on to Halls Creek where John Honner left us to go west. Diary continues-;

---

* *We didn't realize that crocodiles frequent that part of the river.*

John spoke to Father Mc Guire on the wireless at the A.I.M.* hospital. He said he would meet us at Sturt Creek. Two A.I.M. nurses run the hospital on their own. Beer is 8/- a bottle at pub.

Came through low spinifex-covered stony hills. Gullies very rough - had to dig here and there to get car across. Had surveyors behind us; they pushed us through one sand bog. Met Mick Quilty as we passed through Ruby Plains. We came to Billiluna Station then two miles further on to Sturt Creek where a mineral research party of eight welcomed us to lunch in their well-equipped gauzed-in tent. Waited here for Father McGuire but he didn't come. We camped.

Next day:
Waited, then back to Billiluna, talked to a boring contractor who had been through to Balgo. He told us where to go to cross the creek (which was still running strongly and very wide). We started out with Jerry (manager of Billiluna) in jeep to escort us over the bad part. We were met by a Balgo jeep. Fr.McGuire had attempted to get over the previous day but couldn't find a crossing .We had much fun and games going miles, avoiding wet bogs; got madly sand-bogged thrice. Just as well there were plenty of pushers on the Balgo vehicle. Came into real desert - mile upon mile raw red spinifex covered sand.

The lights of Balgo were like a miracle in the desert. A steak dinner was awaiting our arrival. Our trek from the East had taken eight or nine days. I really don't know what I'd expected - perhaps kerosene lanterns and dirt floors. But no. Here were functional buildings, a large generator illuminating the whole Mission complex. My education was to begin.

---

*Australian Inland Mission

Balgo Mission

If you were to take a bird's eye view of Balgo mission in 1967 it was not unlike a rolled out Aboriginal painting on canvas. There was orange rippled sand dotted with pale green spinifex while intersecting the picture were squiggly watercourses lined with white stemmed snappy gums. A collection of iron roofs glinted in the sun. In front of these were small squares of green lawn. These were arranged in a large semi-circle around the concrete basketball courts and gravel playing field. Back from these conventional buildings was a series of transitional houses with tin roofs, half stone walls and outside fireplaces.

Besides these "modern" places were the traditional whirleys consisting of Spinifex placed over a framework of branches - the only homes the old people would use, along with a bevy of skinny faithful dogs.

This was New Mission. The old mission had been established in the 1930's, later abandoned for this better site with a plentiful supply of good bore water. Father Raible, a German priest, had arrived in the Kimberley in 1928 after serving as an army chaplain in Africa in W.W.I. Forthright in his opinion on the plight of the Aboriginal people, he said the state had been "built on the bones of the Blacks, who are the real owners of that country". He aimed to establish a mission and proclaim the Gospel to the nomads. On horseback he ministered to people scattered across the Kimberley. It was ten years before the desert location of Balgo was decided upon.

The iron roofs of Old Mission were taken for re-use when building New Mission. Unfortunately, inroads of wind and weather have left the red antbed buildings of Old Mission in ruins. Phillip Cox, an Aboriginal from Beagle Bay Mission, helped set up the original mission. Here I quote from some of his memories:*

1939.

We drove 1000 head of sheep, 50 goats, a team of donkeys, horses and 5 camels; I think we got 2 camels later. Dick Smith had trained the camels; we could not have got anywhere without him. Starting out, we travelled along the Wolf River, going about 8 to 10 miles a day, depending on the water. One night we might have a dry camp, another night camp beside water. When we got to Sturt River we settled there for a few weeks. We were joined there by Father Alphonse and the rest of the people from Rockhole. I remember one day after saying the rosary, [we said plenty of prayers] Brother Stephen, myself and one of the boys walked in a line towards the billabong holding our sticks for divining. Mine gave a jump. I called the others and sure enough, after two days digging, we got good water in that spot. It was our answer to our prayers. Further on: It was really hard work sinking the wells. I remember setting up the winch which had only one handle, a long wire rope with a bucket on the end. We'd lower the person going down to fill the bucket with mud and wind them up again. We'd use gelignite too. We'd go down, lay the sticks with a long fuse, light it, then get the boys to pull us up quick. Bro. Stephen almost always did that job. One day, after lighting the fuse the boys were hauling him up when the handle on the winch broke. He was a big man, Bro. Stephen - he fell down to the bottom and the boys were calling 'Brother you O.K?" He began yelling for the

* *Part of a letter written to people at Balgo 1995.*

boys to pull him up. The Aboriginals came running. They wrapped the rope, a wire rope mind you, round their bodies and pulled and pulled. God must have been with him. Just as he got to the top, the thing 'Blew' - but instead of the rock and dirt blowing out the top it exploded down into the well. When we went down later it was all ash down there. Brother really suffered after that; the fumes from the explosion got him. It was lucky though, as the explosion blew out the stakes holding the winch. They fell across the hole, missing Bro. He was so lucky. God was with him!

1940.

Brother Alphonse worked hard out there, cutting posts, helping with the mills. I used to get annoyed when he would go down the well, and one day said "Father, that's not your job; you should be preaching and teaching the people their prayers". I thought that wasn't a job for a priest, but Father took no notice.

During the time we were there, there were no radios, no trucks - only camel or horseback. Every one or two months we'd ride to Halls Creek to collect mail.

Most of the mission buildings were basic and serviceable, constructed generally of galvanized iron. The simple church was the most aesthetic of the mission buildings; it was built of the local colourful sandstone and had an imposing bell-tower.

Away to the south an amazing vista opened up. Once an inland sea, we called this breakaway country The Pound. Mesas sculptured by wind and time, rising from limestone flats glistening purple in the sun. Thousands of acres strewn with fossilized rocks of ancient seashell, bounded by the 'jump-up', shoreline of the vanished sea. Here were hidden rockholes overhung with limestone, bearing ochre paintings of the dreamtime.

The horses ran in The Pound and did well there. Creek channels running off the hills provided waterholes early in the year after "the wet". It became necessary to find a bore site later on.

At Balgo lived more than two hundred Aboriginal people who had come in from the desert over the years from 1939 when mission was established, till recent years. These were Gogadga speaking people. Blindness was endemic among the old people, commonly known as "Sandy Blight" it affected both white and black people in early days. As living conditions improved, less whites were affected but remote Aborigines continued to be hurt by the disease, possibly increased as they gathered in larger groups. Heat, wind and dust were part of the problem. Father Frank Flynn, an ophthalmologist working in the Northern Territory, had established a treatment program using sulphonamide drugs and eye ointments to combat trachoma in the Northern Territory. (It was he who was was instrumental in getting aforementioned David Kerrin from Tennant Creek into St.Edmunds School for the Blind in Sydney). Other pioneers in the field were working in South Australia and Western Australia. Professor Fred Hollows led a survey team in 1976 initially in the arid zones, including Balgo, treating Trachoma and associated eye conditions. My nephew Jack Waterford was part of the team for two years, organizing and writing up a report on the program.

For a time Margerie Baldwin was a member of the Hollows team. Though I never met her I include briefly her story*: She

---
* *I read in an article in the Sydney Morning Herald*

was one of the mixed blood children born in the North. Her father was a well known Kimberley cattleman who managed Christmas Creek and later Go Go station near Fitzroy Crossing for the pioneer Emanuel family. Her mother was a tribal Aboriginal, Fanny. Till she was five, Margerie had the run of the 'big house' and went around the station with her father. But West Australian government policy was to take half caste children and send them to school or mission. To prevent this Vic arranged for his daughter to go to his mother's cattle station in the Gulf country of Queensland, where she was adopted by an Aboriginal couple, the Baldwins. When the time came Mrs. Jones sent her grandaughter to boarding school in Herberton. Margerie spent her school holidays with her grandmother. Not until, as a well educated, well travelled young woman of thirty-two, working for the Trachoma team did Margerie meet with her mother at Fitzroy Crossing.

Balgo bought bulls from Christmas Creek near Fitzroy Crossing, getting every available vehicle with crate in action to transport sixty bulls for our breeding stock.Tim Emanuel generously threw in six of his best bulls in support of the mission plans.

There were four St John of God nuns at Balgo when we arrived :- Sr. Francis who ran the hospital; Sr. Veronica who cooked and taught the girls; Sr. Anthony, who buzzed about in her Willys jeep with trailer, and looked after the dormitory and laundry; while old Scottish Sr. Andrew was in charge of the kindergarten. Her brown-skinned little angels of the desert sang nursery rhymes with a Scottish accent!

To quote Banjo Paterson, "Flowing beards were all the go" I noticed, as we walked in to the whitefellas' dining room. I was the only woman, here with my two little boys in tow. I blush to think of the faux pas I made those early days in my naivety; I made a few. Father John McGuire presided over this always interesting group, keeping us in touch with the outside world, as he came in from the early morning "scheds" and telegrams on transceiver radio. The men, who embellished many a story over a meal here, included two St John of God brothers, a welder, a mechanic, windmill men and bore drillers, geologists, mineral explorers, sometimes anthropologists, travelling station people and the single teacher (the married teachers having a house apart). To have twelve or fourteen around the table was quite the norm. All had their stories, some escaping painful memories, others, the law. There were men who worked consistently for three months, then off to town to break out (with their skins cracking, it was said) their hard earned cheque going in a haze of alcohol.

Father McGuire was the administrator. Well known around the Kimberleys, always ready to share a yarn and a whisky in the pannikin around the campfire. "I really hate the stuff, but I'm working on acquiring a taste for it" he would say to my children.

On the Mission, his rule was absolute. It suited those times, when tribal trouble could erupt in a spear fight at the drop of a hat. Though his word was law, it was benign, and dished out with abundant humour and patience. As he drove his landrover round the mission or out bush, there was always a bunch of kids hanging all over it giving directions with movement of lip or a wordless point of arm. He had an affinity with the more troublesome young people. "More spirit", he'd say.

Fr. McGuire was one of a large family from a dairy farm in Victoria. Having put his age up, he joined the army until he was discharged for pulling on a strike over the poor quality of food. He was president of the Y. C. W. (Young Christian Workers), his labour leanings and strong ideas on social justice eventually prompting him to join the Pallotines and become a priest. He was sent to Rome to do his studies, a far cry from his desert ministry at Balgo.

He had a great love of good horses and also had connections with the racing fraternity in Victoria. The horse breeding industry at Balgo was the beneficiary of some well known sires (gifts from generous Victorians), *Basin Street* and *Palm Boy* among them.

The Kimberley region was blighted by the dreaded walkabout disease in horses. This was caused by the Crotaleria plant, which, in certain dry conditions, horses ate. They were then doomed to walk and walk until they dropped. Horses with "walkabout" were known to walk into trees or even out to sea. Being free of this plant, Balgo bred horses to supply for Kimberley stations.

On Balgo, everyone who could work was expected to work. The unwritten policy was for us, the whites, to "work ourselves out of a job," providing useful work to train the young people to be self sufficient over time. Just how much time was a moot point.

Old Mission

Christmas day.

Old Mission buildings made from antbed.

Front - Matt, Conor, John, baby Kimberley, Sean.
Back - Brendan and Norah.

Shearing Shed where blade shears were used when shearing sheep which were shepherded, Dingo's were a problem.

Gordon Downs stockcamp.

Paddy with Sean and Matt.

Matt in camp.

A good catch of bush tucker, Lake Gregory.

Kersh Springs.

Muntja, Nicholas and Sean - Boundary Bore.

Matt and Sean at Little Flower Bore.

Brendan, Donny Milner, Matt, Dominic and Sean,
when building sandstone homestead.

John roping bronco branding.

Sean cooking bush tucker, Matt and Muntja.

John Shoobridge.

Horsebreaking in Sturt Creek roundyard,
Balgo stockmen - Peter Waterford

Our Early Days at Balgo

Balgo's plans to establish a working cattle station was where the Kersh family came into the scheme of things.

Our letter to Bishop Jobst of Broome resulted in our arriving full of idealism and hoping to achieve this. John, with his station experience, was the man for the job. Father McGuire would give someone the responsibility for a job, and let them do it without undue interference. He dealt with all sorts of people and had developed the art of delegating. "That way I am as good as any man on the mission". It was in the days of sexist expressions.

Cattle which had been bought from Billiluna fifty miles to the north, had found their way back to their known country over wet seasons. Few fences existed on the one million-acre runs. Duma Dora yards, strongly built of desert oak from down the Canning, was situated in The Pound where our horses ran. Albert Kelly, a Beagle Bay man and friend of Father McGuire, had come to Balgo to help build the new mission. He had organised the building of these yards. Albert was a man of many parts, spoke three languages - his own native dialect plus English, and German learned from the German missionaries. He played the organ as a hobby.

John's initial job was to get enough working horses together to attend the first round of the Billiluna muster, and with luck pick up some of the wandering Balgo cattle.

John was green to Kimberley ways but using the tried and trusty saddle horses, he and his stockmen yarded the four hundred or so horses, mostly unbroken, into Duma Dora yards. These they sorted through and enough stock horses were drafted off to walk up the fifty miles to Billiluna Pool, where they joined up with the Billiluna stock camp.

Because it had been a record wet season, Lake Gregory, into which Sturt Creek flowed, had spread over a vast area with endless islands and peninsulas, reaching out towards the sand hills. The terrain was treacherously boggy so pack camels were being used to carry the camp gear. Billiluna Johnny looked after them, hobbling them out at night. Camp gear was packed into wooden boxes hung each side of the camel every morning, to walk along to dinner camp. It was John's first experience with these delightful creatures. Like all animals they had their personalities, and no doubt like us, the odd sulky moments. "The horses didn't like the smell of the camels. They would snort and shy away" John said. "And spit! The buggers. You'd have to watch your step loading them, they could spit accurately."

Gerry Adamson was manager of Billiluna. He and his wife Nola had seven children to whom Nola taught correspondence school, education being among the 1000 tasks of the station "Missus". Previously Gerry had been in Alice Springs where he met, in a pub, John Shoobridge, a retired Tasmanian farmer. John was keen to have a look at the Kimberleys and Gerry offered him the job of camp cook.

John Shoobridge was one of the inimitable characters we had the pleasure of knowing. Among others whom my husband met on that first muster were Bob Savage, who was to take the road mob and drove the bullocks over five hundred miles to Alice Springs railhead. Bob later took up Supple Jack Station in the Northern Territory. Big Johnny Watson from Port Hedland way was there, as well as the Billiluna Aboriginal stockmen.

Back at the Mission, the Sisters had lost no time in appointing me to run the kindergarten. This was a surprise to me - my skills at counting games and singing nursery rhymes were nil. Sister Andrew was taking a long awaited journey home to Scotland, and though I couldn't fill her shoes I was given her job. My admiration knows no bounds when I think of Sister Andrew and the Irish sisters who left their home countries to come to this far-off place. The contrast even for Australian women from Victoria must have been daunting enough.

Grocery orders were made twice a year: 150 pound bags of flour by the dozen (we made all our own bread), Ceylon tea in tinfoil-lined plywood chests, 5-gallon tins of jam, Californian Poppy hair-oil, chewing tobacco, tinned dry potato (atrocious stuff!) and tinned cheese and butter, to name a few of the goods shipped from Perth to Derby or Wyndham, four hundred miles still from Balgo. Our mail arrived fortnightly by plane. No telephones, our communication was via the transceiver radio, public to the whole northwest. We knew what went on – whether it be a medical problem, romance or scandal.

There is a story of a Kimberley man who was not great at spelling and didn't know the phonetic alphabet used when reception was bad. It was wet season and snakes were making a nuisance of themselves. Old mate was on the radio sending a telegram to order a gun from the store in Derby. Radio base couldn't hear him clearly, so requested he spell it out. "I want a gun – G for Jesus, U for onion – N for pneumonia" he shouted into the speaker.

My work at the kindy was made smooth by the capable hands of sixteen year-old Nancy. One morning I saw her hurrying the little ones to class by tossing a handful of pebbles at their heels. They scurried along in giggles. Nancy knew the routine of the songs and counting games and would light a heater for the chocolate milk at mid morning. Two year-old Sean joined in the activities while baby Matthew was the centre of attention as he sat on a rug and took it all in. Among my treasures are letters from Nancy. As a promising student she was sent south to training school, and wrote to us regularly in a neat hand. A teenage girl, homesick for Balgo and friends, enquiring about her contempories - who was boyfriend to whom? Nancy was getting a guitar and having lessons. Her letters always included a word for our children. I visualize her now, on the basketball court in print cotton dress, dark arms and legs flying, looking over her shoulder with a saucy smile for the boys. Nancy died, we heard, as a young woman, I think from diabetes.

A letter here from Nancy to our children, when she went to training school in the south:

Dearest Sean and Matthew and Conor and Brendan,

How are you all I hope well also your baby boy. I was glad to see you all when I was home I must say you all have grown up into a very big boys and smart ones too I hope you all behave for your mam and dad. I am well down here and sometimes its very hot. I have not seen Mr. and Mrs. Heath yet but if I do I will tell them all about you all. I still have the photos of you Sean and Matthew and nothing of Brendan and Connor and baby but I hope you ask your mom to send me one of you, will you. And do you go for a swim sometimes with the stockboys? As mom said the lake is full now. I hope to hear from you all one day and also you must tell me when your birthdays are and how old you are. Well I must close now as I have to start my dinny, hows your dog?

With all my love and best wishes for 1973 xxxx
May God bless you all.
Yours loving friend
Nancy Lee

P.S. You are all bigger enough to look after your mom and dad now. Anyhow I hope you do love xxxxx
N.L.

Until our pre-fabricated house arrived on the back of a truck we stayed in the two- bedroom hospital. Right from the start, John was away most of the time. When we left the East we had no idea of the magnitude of the operation of bringing the necessities of life to a place so isolated as Balgo. All goods were shipped on the coastal steamers, calling at ports along the way from Perth to Derby, or Wyndham. The mission semi trailer toiled along the hazardous road five hundred miles to Derby or four hundred miles north to Wyndham a couple of times a year to collect these loadings. Alternately there was five hundred miles plus of sand and dirt south west over the Tanami to Alice Springs.

On hearing by telegram from the bishop of the imminent arrival of the Kersh family, Father Mac, not one to waste time, had ordered from Perth a pre-fabricated house. We arrived long before this loading, all unknowing the turmoil the bishop's message had caused. Sister Francis arranged for us to use the hospital.

I looked at the hospital room, basic and clinical. We unpacked a station wagon load of gear, our worldly goods. Set up Matt's cot, transforming the austere space into cluttered homeliness. Later when our kit home was built, Muntja was my companion. Our home was erected half a mile from the main mission on the bank of a dry creek with spindly white snappy gums softening the red gravel backdrop. With John away with stockwork, Muntja and her husband, Mosquito, were appointed our family guardians. Spreading their swag each evening outside our simple abode and building a fire for their billy of tea - an even simpler abode under starry skies. Muntja helped with my washing in the mornings. With ready smile and expressive hands she explained much to me. I wish I had understood more as she was a real communicator, using a mixture of Gugadga and English. Once, John's sister Jennice, was visiting - a glamourous young woman who had a hair piece added to her long tresses. This she shampooed and pegged on the clothes line one evening. Next morning, hearing a screech from outside, we rushed out to find a shaking Muntja pointing at this thing on the line "Missus! Missus!" We explained that it was not a scalp, Jennice showing her how it worked. Muntja collapsed in laughter - the ways of white women a mystery indeed. Muntja's eldest son, Gregory, joined the stock camp when he left school. A good looking charmer, he sang Slim Dusty songs and wrote some of his own. The sad strains of Trumby who "couldn't read or write" and the haunting tale of "Saddle Boy" must have been composed to be sung by the camp fire.

I was getting to know the white residents of Balgo. There were government teachers, Don and Wendy Lee, and Mark Neville. Mark later trained as a geologist and in the course of his ventures found two gold mines and discovered also the biggest copper deposit in Western Australia; it was named after him. Mark was drawn into politics becoming a member of parliament. He felt aboriginal affairs were going down the wrong track. Self determination was the catch cry of the day, but he could see, in reality kids were getting damaged in the process. He retains a connection and interest in Aboriginal education, publishing a series of adult education books which are widely used by Aboriginal communities, also prisoners who have missed out on learning to read.

There was Brother Michael, who drove trucks for loadings; Brother Wally, the general handyman; the four St John of God Sisters; a mechanic, and Ukrainian Johnny, the resident welder, who told me heart-stopping stories of the war. He had walked all over Europe surviving the war. Johnny was one of four men who first dug for gold at the Granites in the Tanami Desert. A more remote a place could hardly be imagined. It was abandoned because of distance and other problems, but Johnny always maintained there was gold to be taken out at the Granites. History has proved him correct as the mining company is presently working a massive open cut, and miners fly in and fly out as fortunes are made. Last time we saw Johnny (on a trip to the Kimberley in 1994) he was prospecting on Alice Downs Station, living in his bush camp, his Landrover and bulldozer under a tree, immaculate pots and pans lined up by his fire. He was straight as a die at seventy years of age.

Brian McCoy and Pat Mullins, two Jesuit students, came to Balgo in the course of their years of study. We were present at their ordinations years later in Melbourne. Brian has since spent many years with the people of Balgo, becoming an expert on men's health among other things, Pat worked at Turkey Creek in the Kimberley, then Darwin and now in an underprivileged part of Sydney.

Les Stansfield, ex army, windmill man and jack of all trades taught us the rudiments of Bridge playing while working out at the homestead. Sitting round our table late at night with the generator thumping in the distance we must have looked an odd collection. I had imagined it was posh English ladies who played this game: Tony, every bit a bushranger in looks, travelling bush worker; Mick and Bindy from the Alice, who worked a drilling rig were some of the changing population. At the Mission it was customary to play cards at the teacher's house on Friday, many a late night we spent gambling for matches or pennies, and sorting out the world's cares, as Sean, a starfish, one arm slung across Matt's peaceful form, slept on a rug on the floor.

Reception on radio out there was only possible on Radio Australia so our news was worldwide. At Cape Canaveral, scientists had their eyes on the moon. In Vietnam, war was devastating people's lives. We were very much removed until Barry, one of our volunteers, was called up. Suddenly this far away war was not so far from home.

*   *   *   *   *

Wedding at Gordon Downs

An invitation came over the two-way, inviting us to attend Milton and Madeline's wedding at Gordon Downs. Milton Hayes was head-stockman while his brother, Ralph, was manager - before going on to manage Wave Hill in the Territory. Madeline was teaching correspondence school to Ralph and Thea's three boys.

Gordon Downs was an establishment comprising a large Aboriginal population and numerous white staff. The station homestead was the hub around which the work program revolved.

Rounds of cattle mustering were constant through the dry season: Branding calves, drafting bullocks for sale, keeping everyone busy from daylight till dark. The image I have from that time of station life, is of efficiently running active places. The 240-volt engine for lights would be cranked up before daylight as the kitchen girls wandered in to begin their day. They set the yeast for baking large quantities of bread and cutting up "big mobs" of beef, the staple diet.

The manager's wife oversaw everything. This included running a daily clinic to attend to coughs and colds. For something more serious, consulting over the transceiver with the flying doctor.In the old-style laundry, complete with copper and Mother Potts irons, would be five or six women doing the washing and ironing, while their small children crawled or played about in the vicinity. Stress non existent, it was not part of our language those days, nor was there time to think about it; plenty of banter and laughter accompanied the work.

Spacious lawns surrounded the homestead with stately ghost gums here and there. In the shade a couple of old aboriginal men stood rolling a smoke or leisurely raking a few leaves. Bougainvillea added splashes of colour to the white painted corrugated iron of the homestead. Shades of a colonial era – the dining room table at Gordon Downs had a punkah, a large swinging fan worked by a cord hanging above it. It was not used in our day.

Getting to Gordon for the wedding proved to be a fair effort. During the wet, Balgo had three inches of rain but Sturt Creek Station had received 18`inches. Balgo teachers, Don and Wendy Lee, John, our two small boys and I travelled to Sturt Creek. I was pregnant with my third baby. We arrived at Sturt for lunch with manager Rod Russell.

Sturt Creek was still running waist deep, so we were to take an old track which Rod knew. En route our radiator had burst so John and the Lees took the station blitz, while Sean, Matt and I, priviledged because I was pregnant, were to travel in the relative comfort of Rod's landrover with two jackaroos on the back. The trip seemed to take forever, vehicles slowly rattling over bumpy terrain, skirting swampy country remaining from the wet - losing the track completely at times in the high grass. There had been good rain all along during the wet season and we were going north where the average rainfall increases. After thirty bone-shattering miles we made camp. No sooner had we thrown swags down and gathered sticks for a fire, we knew it would be an uncomfortable camp. Mosquitos swarmed about us. We huddled round the smoky fire trying to escape the onslaught, as we munched corned beef and mission bread. We were sweltering. Smoke kept the mosquitoes away and brought tears to my eyes. Unable to stand the heat, I'd move away from the smoke and fire, only to be driven back within minutes, slapping hopelessly at those persistant mossies. Throughout the long night the little boys awoke again and again crying fretfully. Someone would throw a few more sticks on the fire. I could only wrap my babies to ward off the bites, feeling vexed and helpless, unable to comfort them, wishing for the dawn. At picininny daylight we were packed and on our way continuing along the almost non-existant track. Five miles from Gordon Downs, we came to half a mile of wet road. Rod ploughed through, but John, after bogging the blitz, decided to leave it there. It was so good to get to the station and find that Thea had beds for all the women guests and even a cot for Matt. Men camped in their swags. All had been gathering at the station in the preceding days.

The wedding took place on the lawn in the evening. Madeline looked a picture in that garden setting, long shadows of the eighty-odd guests back lit by a golden Kimberley sunset. Two of her sisters-in-law and a nursing friend were bridesmaids. Celebrations continued well into the night as we danced on a square of concrete. Sleepy children were put to bed when they could no longer hold their eyes open. Though, they too, didn't give up without a battle, so much excitement in one day.

While everyone was together next day, a race meeting was held. Wendy, the children and I came home with Rod on a different road. And waded the Sturt Creek in the dark, feeling our way with bare feet in thigh-high running water, while carrying Sean and Matt on our shoulders. We spent the night at Sturt Creek. John and Don didn't get back till early morning.

*   *   *   *   *

Brendan's Arrival

Sister Francis ran the two bed hospital at the Mission. Patients sat each morning on the verandah waiting for medical attention. Francis took it all in her stride, stitching wounds or administering medicine "or a bit of T.L.C." as she said.

John came in to the hospital once with a gash above his eye where a gate had hit him. Some time had elapsed since the injury and the initial numbness had worn off, so when Francis bathed the wound with antiseptic and began stitching, John nearly hit the roof. The Aboriginies were much more stoic.

Sister Francis had to deal with everything from the mundane to the drastic - from the everyday "guts-ache" or sore eyes, to the results of a tribal fight over an infringement of tribal law. Perhaps a spear wound through the thigh, or the dreadful stone-battered skull self-inflicted in mourning. I have since thought there may be something in this therapy for grief, when nothing else seems to help.

The flying doctor made routine trips to Balgo along with station visits. Our little boys received their triple antigen when their turn came. We met Robyn Miller who became known as the Sugar Bird Lady because she brought the polio vaccine. All the children lined up at the hospital and were handed a cube of sugar with pink liquid vaccine dripped onto it. Robyn, a fair haired girl, was a trained nurse and pilot, the daughter of Mary Durack and Horry Miller, aviation pioneer and co-founder of MacRobertson Miller Airline. Robyn kept diaries and her story *Flying Nurse* tells of her flights of mercy, often in bad weather, to rescue seriously ill people on isolated stations. She also co-piloted several R.F.D.S. planes from America with Dr Dicks, whom she married. After her untimely death from cancer at age thirty-five, *Sugar Bird Lady* was published by her husband and her mother, with stories from her diary. A heroic Australian. I would love to see her story on the school syllabus.

When in late pregnancy with Brendan, I was woken by a dull aching pain in my lower back. I was worried. The notes with the Flying Doctor chart *Assisting with a Station Birth* alarmed me. I was pretty ignorant and recalled hemorrhaging for weeks after Matthew's birth, not knowing it was not normal. John was out in the stock camp, the little boys cosily asleep in their cots and the ululating murmer from the Aboriginal camp had long ceased. Another pain hit me. "Midnight" the luminous hands of the clock on the kitchen shelf told me. I didn't want to drive up and wake Sister Francis at this hour. Outside I saw the embers of Muntja's and Mossy's campfire glow comfortingly. Again the dull pain assailed me. My mind argued with itself 'Baby is not due this soon. Go to sleep! Ouch! Should I drive up and wake Francis? No I wouldn't - it's a false alarm'. I began timing the pains just in case, then must have dozed off. All a false alarm as it turned out. Nevertheless, I mentioned it next day to Francis and she was only too keen to pack me off to Derby on the next plane. She was an experienced nurse, but it had become government policy to send all pregnant women to Derby hospital to have their babies. She certainly didn't need to be dealing with a white woman (far more cosseted than any black woman).

The Sisters looked after Sean and Matt till John's mother came up and took over the care of her grandchildren. A mission truck was already on its way back from Alice Springs when it started to rain. A new International truck had been ordered for the stock camp and John was to collect it. He was able to hitch a flight with a Geophysical mob to meet his mother in " the Alice," and take delivery of the new truck. The weather was so overcast they flew at the height of just one hundred feet most of the way, at Mount Wedge going through a gap in the hills, an exciting ride. Meanwhile the mission truck was battling to get along, bogging over and over. The driver and a few stockmen unloading, digging their way out of that morass only to sink hopelessly a few miles further on.

John, having met his mother in the new 4-wheel drive truck (with thirty hundredweight of lick for the cattle on board), were on their way back. They caught up with the mission truck which had been days on the road. These weary travellers were persuaded to jump on the back of the new vehicle which was more able to negotiate the boggy country. Among the troughs, pipes and general gear on the mission truck, were thirty cartons of beer. The cartons had all disintegrated in the rain, so bottles had to be stacked and restacked. The remarkable part of the story was that the driver had a real weakness for the drink, and yet with the trials and tribulations of the trip, had not cracked one bottle open.

Derby, five hundred plus miles north west of Balgo, was an eye opener to me. It is situated on King Sound near the mouth of the Fitzroy River, approximately seventeen hundred miles by sea from Perth. It was a cattle shipping port for the west Kimberley. The tide rises up to thirty-five feet so that the jetty projects way out to sea. At low tide ships sat high and dry by the jetty. There are extensive mud flats, and the odd salt water croc, all around the town. When the tide was in, the mud flats were transformed to a sparkling expanse of Indian Ocean.

While awaiting my baby's arrival, I stayed at the Aboriginal Children's Hostel run by young lay workers from the eastern states and even from overseas. There was beautiful Irish Brede, who enchanted us (and the local policemen) with her wit, and the petite pony-tailed German girl who had volunteered to run the kindergarten. The children from stations lived at the hostel during term attending the local school, returning to their station homes for holidays. The boys and girls had separate dormitories with a communal dining room and shared play time. Work was full on with cooking, washing and the responsibilities of looking after teenage kids. For me it was an enlightening experience, each day bringing its tears, dramas or joys and being handled as cheerfully as possible by all concerned.

I was surprised and overcome to receive a telegram from my mother in N.S.W. telling me she was flying over to stay with me. Norma, who rarely left her beloved Ned's side and the most non-extravagant of people, was to cross literally the width of Australia to be with me. I could hardly contain my excitement when she stepped off the 'plane. Tall elegant and my mum, just knowing how I needed her. We shared a room in the hostel, where my mother was a welcome person with whom the young ones could converse, and appreciate her dry sense of humour and her wisdom.

Sister Damien, (one of the St John of God nuns) had taken me under her generous wing and shown me around. I had the privilege of a trip to the government Leprosarium which the Sisters ran from 1936 until 1986 when it closed. Hansen's disease (leprosy) was able to be treated now by modern drugs. Over the years the Sisters had worked with the people medically and socially, bringing them music, schooling, arts and crafts. I quote from Sister Alphonsus Daly's *Healing Hands:*

"... and so the orchestra grew until, over a period of years, there were no fewer than forty-six violins, six banjos, one cello and a cornet. The rehairing of bows was a major concern, as insects could not be prevented from nibbling at the hairs in the humid heat."

Wondering when my baby would arrive I was a bit lost when Sister Damien invited me on a trip to Broome, calling in at Yeeda on the way, where we lunched with the manager's wife. She had grown up on Fossil Downs near Fitzroy Crossing. At Broome too, the Sisters had a long history, going back to 1908, of teaching and nursing in the multi-racial community. Approaching the old pearling town I saw luggers lying in disrepair among the mangroves. Each, no doubt had its own story of the brave pearl divers who risked their lives in search of shell on the ocean floor. Ted Egan's song "Sayonara Nakamora" has all the pathos of the time.

When the Derby native hospital was falling into dilapidation, the decision had been made to abandon it and build a new town hospital which served the whole community. The St. John of God Sisters, who staffed the native hospital, became part of the staff of the new town hospital. Sister Damien was one of these. At the old native hospital, as I stood on the sprawling verandah with its wooden lattice work overlooking the tidal flats, I felt an eerie sadness for times past. I could visualise on the old cane chair a dark-skinned lady in floral dress gazing across the evening water, with banyans whispering in the warm breeze, and the ghosts of nuns in white habits and blue checked pinnies attending the sick.

My mother and I were invited to join the Sisters for a picnic. We took the road out to Camballin on the mighty Fitzroy. Kim Durack, of the pioneering Durack family, had developed the idea of an irrigation farm. It experienced many of the problems of the remote northwest, particularly of pests - and distance, always distance. Camballan is now a research station.

Thea Hayes from Wave Hill Station, Northern Territory, was in hospital when I arrived in Derby. She put her nursing experience to use as she awaited transport home by plane. A young American woman, Lauren, was expecting her first baby so we spent time together and compared notes. Her father, Bud Crockett, was a descendant of Davy Crockett of "King of the Wild Frontier" fame. Lauren's family had come from Montana to find their own frontier in the Kimberley of Western Australia.

In due course, my third son, Brendan, made his appearance. Holding my newborn baby was love at first sight. My enchantment never diminished - each child unique, I learned what unconditional love meant truly when I had my own babies. My dates weren't so well worked out, but I am sure Brendan was late – something he has continued, being a sociable person

- always ready for a yarn or to stop on the road to help someone out. A big healthy baby, he was celebrated by the hostel folk and showered with gifts and blessings.

When the next plane was due we were on it – so we did the milk run round the Kimberley stations until we were flying over the now well-known Bungle Bungles. The Kimberley region is a kaleidoscope of colour at anytime. From the air, the great winding rivers and rugged spinifex-dotted landscape is a marvel. Eventually our plane landed on the Balgo airstrip, to be met by the Mission Landrover – numerous kids hanging off it, and Sean and Matt eager to inspect their new brother. A crisis had occurred in the stock camp preventing John's presence, but that is the way it goes. Disappointed, but understanding only too well: I knew thirsty stock took precedence over all else.

Four little boys, Matt, baby Conor,
Sean and Brendan at Duma Dora.

Alan, Sean and Bob.

To The Alice for Peter

It is often said of country people that distance doesn't matter to us. Distance is what we do. However, when you have someone bleeding severely from an accident, or a sick child, or less dramatically, a hundred miles to drive over an indifferent dirt road with no air conditioning, one or another of the children calling out regularly "Dad, Dad can you stop, I'm busting!" distance *does* matter.

There were some interesting trips over the years we spent at Balgo. One such journey happened when my nephew, Peter Waterford, had to be collected from Alice Springs. Peter had flown there from Lightning Ridge - via Sydney to Adelaide, then having caught the Ghan for the steady trip to the Centre. Not long left school, he was coming to help at Balgo.

Wet season was over but so far no-one had made the 530-mile trek to Alice Springs, so the track was an unknown quantity. Looking forward to seeing Peter, and a rare trip to town, the children, John and I set forth in the Landrover, the usual 44's of fuel and water on board as well as swags, tucker and medical kit. We got only as far as the unmarked N.T. border, roughly a hundred miles from the mission, and ran into wet claypans. After a series of bogging and bumping over the spinifex, detouring wet areas, at last we turned back. We left it to dry out for a week or so, and this time John with two stockmen hit the road again in Fr. McGuire's vehicle.

Meanwhile Peter, waiting in the Alice, was running short of money. He rang his father asking for some replenishment. His father promptly told him to find some work. The parish priest obliged, and Peter chipped a stone into shape for a plaque for the Catholic Church. He maintains also, that the garden hedges around Alice Springs were never so well clipped.

John and the boys, travelling towards Alice Springs, stopped, set up the transceiver and called the Mission, reporting they had passed the point where we had previously turned back and were beyond the old Granites gold mine. Sched times were held at certain times of day, so one stopped and set up the radio on the mudguard and stretched the aerial to the highest thing available, maybe a spindly tree, then switched on the radio, hoping to have reception. Each radio had its own call sign, ours was WNE: Whiskey November Echo. Having received John's message I slept easy, hoping they would reach town next day.

In fact, for the travelers, it was trouble from then on, grinding along making thirty and forty mile detours around wet claypans. They reached a stage with water stretching ahead, where they left the landrover to scout around. After a long fruitless walk, John turned around to see a column of smoke rising in the direction in which he had left the vehicle. "Bloody hell, the Landrover!" Heart in his boots, he knew.

What had probably happened was that, while driving cross-country, dry grass had jammed round the hot exhaust pipe under the vehicle. Left standing solitary in a sea of waxy flammable spinnifex, heat off the exhaust must have ignited that matted thatch caught underneath, and in minutes become an inferno. Here I quote from a letter to my parents:

"They came back to see the whole vehicle burned to smithereens, including transceiver wireless, swags, loads of cash (from chaps here wanting things from town). This was about 100 miles from the mission – more than 400 from the Alice".

As they had driven by the Granites (long abandoned gold mine) the day before, they had seen a grader and caravan which had been left there before the wet. The stranded three walked back there. Providentially, there was a transceiver in the van, with a fairly run-down battery and luckily John was just able to make himself heard at Tennant Creek base, hundreds of miles to the east. Tennant Creek heard his faint call and John was able to give them a message to wire the Mission telling of their plight. Resourceful as ever, Fr McGuire sent a wire to Peter in Alice Springs suggesting he go to Conellan's Airline, charter a plane, land at the Granites, pick up the travellers and come on to Balgo.

This is from Peter's end of the story: He received a telegram with instructions to hire a plane, land at the Granites in the Tanami Desert, then proceed to Balgo, signed McGuire (Peter had not heard of McGuire.) Picture the 16-year old boy rocking up at Connellan's Airways with this request. He had the pilots, who had not heard of the Granites, scratching their heads, when senior pilot George Taylor walked in. He had flown over that way and knew the country. So it was with George, that Peter found himself winging his way into the wilderness. "I haven't flown this way for years," remarked Mr.Taylor to Peter "I'll do a few loop the loops, it'll keep us awake!" and this he proceeded to do. He filled Peter in on the local knowledge, and told him that the Granites air strip hadn't been used for thirty years.

John and the boys had scratched out a path, but circling overhead, Peter said there were bushes all over it, and termites' nests two and three feet high. "We might have to dodge these a bit", said George. A skilled bush pilot, he did just that. Bringing the aircraft to a safe standstill, they were met by the three, grinning with relief. Having little luggage to worry about, they were soon off and away to Balgo.

A happy postscript: While overnighting before his return flight to Alice Springs, George Taylor discovered Sister Immaculata, his sister, worked as a nurse at Balgo. They had not seen each other since before the war, when as a boy George had left Perth, joined the Air Force, gone to war and lost family contact.

Thinking of Peter always brings a smile to my face; big of stature and bigger of heart he was a hit with the people of Balgo. He was young, as were most of the stockmen.

Another episode involving Peter was when he and stockmen Rex, Whisky, Gregory and Dreamer were to bring some horses down from Billiluna. There were two routes which they could take. They chose the shorter one straight across the desert. Setting off early, they found the horses wouldn't walk properly; they were not used to obediently going along like the plant horses. It was a slow and frustrating task, the day very hot, and by 1 or 2 pm, they were all feeling totally dehydrated. So much so, that surveying sand hill after sand hill, they thought of just letting the horses go to make their way back from whence they had come. Beginning to worry, as the desert stretched endlessly, tongues literally swelling, their saddle horses flagging, they topped yet another sand hill. "There before us was a watermelon plant, and would you believe it? Three big juicy watermelons!" Peter told me. The boys fell on and devoured them, quenching their awful thirst. "It was a miracle", says Peter. A waterless place, untouched by man it seemed. Do watermelons grow wild? Had a bird dropped the seeds? Who knows? I take the "miracle" view. As the sun crept towards the west, the day gradually cooled down and the horses were brought into Boundary Bore.

Droving Cattle

Having no telephone or any other means of communication but transceiver wireless, I wrote letters home regularly to send on the fortnightly mail plane from Derby. Now and then John wrote with more 'nuts and bolts' information, which my father appreciated. Extract John's letter to my parents describing Balgo:

"The area is 8,040 square miles and for the most, Spinifex country. Though it is soft Spinifex which cattle will eat, also when it is burnt, grasses often come. Then there is some better country on south east and adjoining Northern Territory border. This is where I intend to take the heifers and also erect 20 miles of fence as a paddock to hold them over the wet."

It was arranged that we buy unbranded heifers from Vestey stations as Balgo needed more breeding stock. With Lord Vestey its head, Vesteys were English meat processors owning much country in Australia and the Argentine, as well as numerous meatworks in the Eastern states. They were largely in control of our export beef. Vestey stations did not sell their heifers as a rule, but Father McGuire's friendship with various managers eased the way to make this concession.

A plane was visiting Balgo, so John took the opportunity to hijack the pilot for a couple of hours to fly over the desert seeking a route the cattle could travel from Gordon Downs to

Balgo. Dry stages there would be, no creeks or bores in this un-charted country. From the air a couple of clay pans with water were spotted and a course chosen.

For the droving venture John ordered large rolls of hessian on MacRobertson Miller Airlines (MMA), our mail plane, to use for breaks (night yard) for the young cattle. He would search out a place to camp among a scattering of spindly trees, then drape the hessian from tree to tree with wire to form an enclosure. A revolutionary idea at the time, but today with the advent of helicopter mustering, hessian is commonly used as a wing to haze cattle into a yard.

More from John (prior to droving):

"I arrived home late last night after a week or so up Gordon Downs way. We bled the heifers we are buying, for the Pleuro blood test. As we are south of the Pleuro line all the stock have to be cleared before coming down. From there I took my camp across to the Linacre Racecourse on Nicholson station to help complete the mission camp for next week's races.

Straight after the races we will brand and take delivery of the mob (450) and then walk them 170 miles to here. From here we will then take them down to the southern end. The best of the country on Balgo and never been stocked. It will be about another 130 miles drive."

The children and I stayed at Gordon Downs homestead as the cattle were being organized; we then joined the droving outfit as they walked the ten miles or so a day, till we reached Sturt Creek. For that leg of the journey I was in charge of the cooking. It was basic: plenty of beef cooked in buckets over the fire, and keeping up with bread- making for the hungry drovers. Jam spooned out of a four-gallon tin spread on slabs of fresh bread was the "icing on the cake" so to speak.

Unless the children and I joined up with the stockcamp, we saw little of John. It became a way of life to pack up the children and become part of it. There was a magic to waking up to shuffle and clop clop of hooves, a string of horses darkly outlined on the first light of dawn, as horse-tailer brought them onto camp. Magic in Sean's shout as he made a discovery. "Look Mum! I've found a stone!" cradling a dun coloured rock in his small hand. It looked much the same as other rocks to me, I dropped it into my pocket to add to his precious collection. Or Matt squatting in dappled shade hammering a bloodwood nut with a stone to break open the delicacy inside.

Beautiful, the red brown haze rising until shapes of cattle and horsemen emerge, moving in rhythm as the mob nears dinner-camp. Moments of pure joy at being in this remote place with my family, tracking behind a mob of cattle thrilled my romantic heart, and made up for the hard slug and weariness that accompanied each day's work. The children adapted to whatever was going on. Baby Brendan watched the changing scene through untroubled eyes, while Sean was soon giving directions about how to wash the horses down or where to stack the saddles. We topped a slight ridge one morning to see the expanse of waterhole near Sturt Creek station. Matt's eyes lit up "Water, big mob," he said in tones of wonder. He had not seen a lot of water in his short life. Reaching Sturt Creek, the children and I left the outfit as they headed into the wilderness with its dry stages. After trips like this, I so appreciated water running from a tap, taken for granted at other times. No matter how particular one was, washing in an enamel dish with water from a 44-gallon drum on the back of a truck still left one feeling gritty.

More from John:

"At present young Barry O'Leary and a few of the stock boys are tailing them (cattle) at Boundary bore. We have an option of 110 over at Fitzroy and hope to inspect them early next week, blood test and then truck them here to join the others. The trip down through no-man's land was not without event. The old truck broke down beyond repair one evening over a 25 mile dry stage and left me about 9 miles behind the cattle. I had to walk through the desert that night to get food and water to the boys. The last dry stage, another 25 miles, we did by starting them at 2 a m, walking by moonlight then till about 10 am. From there we walked them into Boundary bore in the evening.

"We have already put an order in next year for a further 500 heifers from Vestey's. A new general manager takes over next month so we hope he is as agreeable. Then, if we can get the last of those on the Billiluna contract, there should be enough to breed up from."

Matt, Sean and Norah at Little Flower bore.

Donny and Patricia "thread the needle" race.

Alan breaking in at Duma Dora yards.

My sister Betty

My mother's letter in my hand, I stood on the hospital verandah. Sister Francis, having tended her daily patients of guts-ache, head-ache or wounds, handed me her medical book. Francis, a trained nurse and St. John of God nun from Victoria, had faithfully run this outpost for years now. The fortnightly plane had landed and delivered me a handful of family letters. My mother's letter had gently informed me of my sister Betty's, (Elizabeth's) illness. She had found a lump on her neck – diagnosed Hodgkin's disease. I had never heard of this. I leafed through the alphabetically ordered book: "Hodgkin's Disease - a form of cancer." I could barely look – but read that it could be slow moving and go on for up to sixteen years, or something to that effect. That is what I latched on to – sixteen years seemed a long time in my youth. It was unthinkable that my beautiful, vivacious, fun sister could be really sick. We had stayed a couple of days with Bet and David and two little ones, Maria and Michael, at their new property at Jugiong in N.S.W. just before travelling west. Betty had been as well as ever. "Anyway" my mind was saying, "she'd beat whatever this thing was".

It was not to be. She courageously lived about four more months, always more concerned for those around her, then graciously left this life in November 1967.

Father McGuire brought the news to us out at our camp at Carrolls Bore, having left the Mission late afternoon, arriving at our camp about two in the morning. Next evening he said Mass, using the back of the Landrover as an altar. The stockmen stood around in a semi-circle in skinny legged jeans and high heeled R.M. boots, their cowboy hatted heads bowed in respect. I put on clean jeans for Betty. A glorious sunset with cattle and mulga silhouetted through the dust was the backdrop.

A fine farewell, but I was pretty numb. I wanted to walk off into the desert by myself, to walk away and keep going, not think, not carry this heavy lump in my chest – but then what? My practical self asserted itself. I just went on making the bread and attending to the demands of small children and a swag of hungry stockmen.

The next mail brought me a stack of letters from the east telling me all about Betty and her big funeral in Young. It was then, back at the Mission, I could give myself over to my private grief. No doubt everyone was kind. Strange – I don't remember much detail. This was still the time of "the stiff upper lip" I guess. We were not encouraged to lay bare our feelings, sadly tucked away inside us.

It was soon after this that my father decided to visit us at Balgo, with my sisters Pat, Fran and Monica, and brother-in-law John Spora. They flew with Bruce Hazelton*, via Uluru and Alice Springs, then north-west to the spot on the map which marks Balgo. John had contracted hepatitis earlier, while attending Billiluna muster, and had been evacuated

---

* *Prior to establishing Hazeltons Airlines, Bruce and his brother Max worked in crop-dusting around the Central West N.S.W. They also ran a charter service – the Kimberley trip was in a Cessna 310.*

to Derby. He was still there when my folks arrived; the bishop flew him back to Balgo a day later. Sean, Matt and I waited by Father Mac's Landrover on the mission airstrip overlooking the Pound. Sean and Matt with mission kids all anticipation.

A murmur of the aircraft is heard, kids the first to notice, then the speck in the sky, skinny black arms pointing, lifting Matt and Sean onto hips and pointing. Hazleton's Cessna 310 banks and comes into a perfect landing. My children and I are embraced by sisters, aunts, Grandad.

What a blessing to have my family come when most needed! Dad loved to see new country, while I relished the idea we could show him, my sisters and brother-in-law our new country.

Building the Homestead

Five million acres native reserve in the Great Sandy Desert gave quite a bit of scope. The challenge for John was to explore and decide the best places to run cattle. Mulga country similar to some territory country was to the south east; it remained to be seen if water could be found there. Bores were drilled. Some proved too salty, others gave good sweet water. Troughs and mills were erected.

A homestead, central to the main stock operation, was needed. Good water was the deciding factor. A site was found about eighty miles from the mission on open sandy spinifex country with an all round view of the horizon. We could see the blue shape of Mt. Tracey away to the east. To the south, on cold mornings the shimmering vision of Middleton's low hills projected upwards like fortresses - a mirage, only to disappear over the curvature of the earth in full sunlight.

Mention of Middletons bore, jars me into recalling a difficult task I had to do. The children and I were doing a routine water check of mill and trough. As we drove up to the windmill, my heart sank to see a cow down and half bogged. Her ribs were showing through her hide and crows had taken one eye. I walked towards her to see what could be done. In fright at my approach, she somehow struggled to her feet, facing me mutely. Then tottered and fell once more into the muddy slush of the tank overflow. There was nothing for it but to shoot her. Otherwise it would be a lingering death at the mercy of crows or dingos. I had learned to use a rifle at an early age, so steeled myself for a job that had to be done. Making sure the children were well behind me I took the rifle from the Toyota cab and stood back for a clear shot. Insert the bullet, cock the rifle, pull the trigger. Bang! The cow didn't die. "Oh, Heck!" I thought "This darned thing!" I had never used a rifle with a telescopic sight before. I had hit the cow in the wrong place. Crying my eyes out, I just had to reload, go right up to the beast and pull the trigger. As graziers, we have to accept that animals die, and nature is often cruel, but I found this bungle just terrible and wished it had been anyone else but me that pulled the trigger.

We set about building the homestead. Gracefully rising from the orange sand were three Bauhinia gums, the only trees in sight. "Let's build round them." I suggested. John thought that was an OK idea. The house plan was roughly L-shaped. One tree would be in the L space, the others on the western side. Imagine my shock one day as I looked across the spinifex to note a small group of the workforce casually chipping away with tomahawks at my precious trees. I flew over to tell the boys that was my garden. From then on, as the house rose stone by stone, the men guarded the trees faithfully, building a little ring of stones around each.

One afternoon a dreadful accident happened. A high steel tankstand was erected, on top a galvanized tank to provide storage for the proposed homestead and stockyards. Ever mindful of cost, this tank was not new, and needed cementing on the inside, to stem the rusted leaks. This particular day, John and one of the boys were 25 feet up in the tank finishing off the job. Inside the tank was a 44-gallon drum they had been standing on. John gave a warning, "Everyone step aside!" He hoisted the drum over the edge of the tank to topple earthwards. The workers below stepped back. Then Terry Murphy, a volunteer from the mission, moved in to mark the spot with the heel of his dusty boot. Too late! To our horror, the drum hurtled down, striking Terry on the head, dropping him to the ground with blood running down his face. We thought he was dead. Oh! In the words of the song, "If you could turn back time." Eighty miles of very steady road lay between us and the mission, and even when he got there - five hundred miles from Derby hospital.

Immediate action needed, someone was appointed to try to contact the mission on the two-way, a mattress was slid into the back of the station wagon and Terry carefully placed upon it. Leaving the children at camp, John, Terry and I began the excruciating journey, feeling every little bump on Terry's behalf. He was still breathing and conscious, on and off. Not knowing what the injury was I just hoped and prayed he would survive. Gentleman that he was, Terry, in his barely audible voice insisted the accident was not John's fault. The Flying Doctor came and Terry spent time in Derby with a broken vertebrae before returning to Balgo, where he continued working, wearing a brace for many months.

The above mentioned tankstand had a few sheets of corrugated iron bolted round the bottom, and a shower installed. What a blessing that was. After hauling black buckets and camp ovens on and off the fire, fighting a losing battle with millions of bush flies and picking up energetic dusty little boys all day, I found a shower washed away more than sticky dirt and grit. It somehow refreshed mind as well as body.

Peter Waterford was an endless source of cheer to stockmen and ourselves over this period. Our little boys padded around tracking lizards and following the saga of a house being built.

I tried in vain to brush the bush flies from their eyes as I prepared food. In clouds of dust old mission trucks churned by, loaded with sandstone quarried from the hills some miles away. One afternoon after a heavy storm a nearby claypan had six inches of water which had run in. I took the children for a swim where they ran naked splashing and sliding in the coffee coloured water, to their hearts delight. Under the fierce sun, they dried off almost as they left the water.

We did get rain over that period, I note in my scratchy diary:

A cyclone was brewing off Broome. Marie Mahood had called on radio to say Rex and Anna were leaving Mongrel Downs to go to the mission; rain started falling; Peter bogged the blitz. Next day diary says "Wet, wet, two and a half inches now, have fire under a tin sheet, cyclone thirty miles west of Derby moving east, some stations deluged with rain, thirteen inches at one place, ten at another.Fourinches has fallen at Billiluna. Les Roche's wedding had to be postponed. Two and a half at mission. Next day: *Cyclone breaking up after heading south east of Broome.*

In the desert, so far inland, we did not get cyclones. Just the rain influence, if we were lucky. The mission ended up with five inches; we had four hundred and eighty points.

My diary dryly goes on:

Still cooking in the rain all day, buckets of rice and spaghetti for men, as we ran out of beef. Now too wet to get a killer.

The beautiful sandstone house was completed, steel stockyards built, an airstrip dragged along a ridge and it became our home. Over the years we became self sufficient, sending cattle off to market. Sounds simple! In reality a huge challenge, with the usual setbacks, dramas and joys.

*   *   *   *   *

Across the Airwaves - Neighbours

Our nearest and only neighbours were across the N.T. border, seventy-five miles to the east, on Mongrel Downs. Joe and Marie Mahood* had taken up this country in partnership with Bill Wilson who owned Billiluna, north of Balgo, and Frome Downs in South Australia. Nothing marked the border between Western Australia and the Northern Territory. The track, red and sandy, wended its way through stands of mulga, twisted branches delivering their meagre shade, and miles and miles of open spinifex and grass country. The symmetry of the 360° horizon was broken only by the rectangular shape of Mt. Tracey, named for Tracey Mahood.

A welcome stop was Mongrel Downs, on rare trips to or from Alice Springs. We would climb from our vehicle, I mostly with a sleeping baby in my arms, his poor little face beaded with perspiration, older children eagerly finding footholds as they clambered from the back of the Toyota. There was always some cold beef and a cuppa at the ready for rare travellers. It was just lovely to sit on the shady verandah stretching limbs after being cramped in the cab of a not-so-well-sprung vehicle.

**Marie became well known and loved for her books and hilarious articles on life in the outback. 'Icing on the Damper' tells the saga of Marie and Joe's pioneering life. Their elder daughter Kim's award winning book 'Craft for a Dry Lake' is a beautiful rendition of growing up in that remote place.*

Marie taught her four children and those of the aboriginal families who worked there, on that gauzed-in verandah. They must have provided material for her children's books later on. The children, imaginative and resourceful, were as handy in the stock camp as in the classroom. A governess was employed to help Marie with the work load - a French girl, Jacquie, with long, dark hair. Bruce Farrands, who was working on Mongrel Downs at the time, was hoping for something like this to brighten his day. He and Jacquie were married and established the road house at Rabbit Flat on the Tanami. They had twin boys. A lonely spot then, now with better roads it is visited by tourist coaches. However, barred windows greet the intrepid visitor; troubles with drink-charged patrons have caused these stern measures.

Much later, in 1990, on their Queensland station Joe Mahood was tragically killed in a chopper while mustering cattle.

To continue south east from Balgo en route to Alice Springs: Malley and Oriel Brown and children were at Chilla Well. Oriel, was a Palm Island girl, and Malley, one of Len and Betty's sons from Billiluna. Malley had the distinction of being one of the Canning Stock Route drovers. The Canning was surveyed by Albert Canning in the early 1900's to move cattle from the Kimberley nearly 900 miles through the Great Sandy Desert to the railhead at Wiluna. An infamous route where prospectors, heading for gold at Halls Creek, disappeared in the wilderness. Some perished for lack of water, others at the point of a spear. Canning had erected wells at native soaks. Here drovers had to draw water, using a wooden frame to lever the galvanized bucket up and swing it around to fill the trough, a painstaking job with hundreds of cattle to water. It was a hazardous droving route when Malley, a boy, sat behind the travelling mob, the desert ahead stretching into infinity. Len Hill, mentioned elsewhere, had also helped take mobs down the Canning as a fifteen-year old, writing his diary in lead pencil as the cattle plodded onwards.

*   *   *   *   *

Memories Unwrapped

Writing about people we met over the years is tricky, especially with my faulty memory. There have been many wonderful people who make life an interesting journey. Too numerous to do them justice, I mention a few Balgo people of our time.

Old Sunfly and his much younger wife, Bye Bye. Sunfly crafted child-sized boomerangs from mulga for our boys and decorated them in ochre yellow, white and red. Dominic, a Balgo identity - deaf, but so able to express himself in action and gesture. When voting rights came in, government men came to Balgo to explain what voting was all about. The assembled population was sitting on the ground to listen to the speech. When it was over your man from Canberra singled Dominic out, his face being the most responsive in the group.

With the advent of voting rights in 1967, full wages were made mandatory. Many stations could not afford to pay a big population full wages. People began to drift into towns. All these people from their tribal country with their own language were thrust into the twentieth century. Many were adversely affected, as innocents confronted by modern life, drink and materialism, unable to cope. Along dirt tracks of the interior are stark reminders of this dislocation, symbolized by cars broken down, burnt out hulks - skeletons in red sand. This,

I think, was the end of the "old days"; not necessarily all good old days, of course. Voting rights and other rights were long overdue but change brought so much calamity. On the stations everyone had a role. Health care was catered for, usually by "the Missus" who ran a daily clinic, anything from minor ailments to severe accident. Tucker was supplied, plus clothes, tobacco and the ubiquitous California Poppy hair oil. It may sound like a cliché, but what I saw on (mainly company) stations with Aboriginal populations of up to eighty people, prior to full wages, was that people seemed to be happy. The prime job of stock work employed most of the young men, while girls and women worked round the house, old men in the garden dreaming. "No different to slaves" a visitor from the South said, to which the station manager drily replied, "Making slaves of these fellers would be a miracle". The manager was one who had the greatest appreciation of and rapport with Aboriginal people and spoke their language.

As I write I see in imagination a 'housegirl' languidly sloshing a mop of sudsy water along the shady verandah while the 'kitchen girl' kneading bread shouts, teasing about one of the stockmen: "That boy, he bin lookin at you. Youai!" From the mopper, a musical giggle as she hides her long eyelashes behind slim brown fingers. "Paternalistic" some chided, for the rather strict routine of work every day. Kids were expected to go to school; it wasn't an option. English, in which they did school, learning to read and write, was their second language. Town kids sometimes scoffed at Balgo kids for their "top English". They didn't learn Pidgin from the nuns.

Change had to come of course, but how great a leap for people in tune with the sun, moon and seasons, to the rush and scramble, so much part of today's society.

John Shoobridge came to work at Balgo as a volunteer and took over the vegetable garden. John, from a pioneering family in Tasmania, was a retired grazier. Leaving his farm in the care of his sons, he had come north. He wanted to give something back to the Aboriginal people. He came year after year, returning to Tasmania over the wet season.

Under his care, with mission boys to help, the garden thrived. He chose to live humbly in the tin shed near the bore, with the 20ft Comet mill blade turning in the wind nearby.

Always a welcome and a mug of tea on offer when we stopped by. On one occasion we pulled in on our way out to the station. Sean and Matt jumped off our truck to explore the garden. John Shoobridge told them they could try anything, but strictly warned them not to touch the chillies. What a challenge! The children soon found the chilli plants with their tempting red fruit. Of course they grabbed a handful and stuffed them into their mouths – then came running back to us yelling – unable to hide their guilty deed. These chillies were of the hottest variety, and forty years later Sean claims his mouth was burning for a week. I must add that Sister Veronica's chilli sauce was a hot favourite at the men's table; years of alcohol must have dimmed their taste buds I feel.

John would load us up with produce from the garden as we took our leave. He loved his Victorian AFL football team, the Bombers, and had a good hand at poetry. He lived till a great age on Bruny Island, keeping a wide correspondence with his many friends. A letter in my box here has a postscript on it reading "Be good Boys. Look after your mother. I'm talking to you, Sean and Matt". He has gone to his reward now – bless him.

Halls Creek Ro-De-O
by John Shoobridge

*Take a "Mulla Bulla" bullock
and a "Flora Valley" colt,
Take the bursting lungs and leather,
take the hooves that jar and jolt,
Take the men who ride for pleasure
and the men who ride for "dough"
Then you've got the lot together
at the "Halls Creek" ro-de-o.*

*Some get courage from the bottle;
some are keen to meet the test,
With that real red badge of courage
planted firmly in their breast,
All are welcome if they're willing
and are masters of the Fate,
But the weak are always weeded
at the final drafting gate.*

*And there stands "Retribution"
the rodeo feature horse,
His sire they say was "Falling Star",
his dam the mare "Remorse".
As yet by man unmastered
with head held proud and high,
He has ruined reputations
from the Fitzroy to Negri.*

Mick and Bindy from around Alice Springs were among many bushmen who passed through. They worked the drilling rig. The rig was a percussion drill or "mud puncher" as they called it, four-wheeled, mostly timber braced with steel. It looked a monotonous job working round the clock, hand on the cables noting each beat of the motor or change in quality of rock coming up. They lived tough lives away from their families much of the time. I was touched by their thoughtfulness when they came back from Halls Creek and presented me with one of those sturdy twin-tub washing machines, guaranteed to remove dirt from work clothes. Until then it had been all hand washing in concrete tubs. Another time, camped at Carroll's bore, Mick and Bindy had their camp adjacent to ours. One of the men was bitten by a cheeky (poisonous) snake out on the fence line. John had to take him in to the Mission. The little boys and I were sharing a billy of tea around the campfire that night with Mick and Bindy. Talk inevitably turned to snake stories, each one more spine-chilling than the last. I leaped in fright when a Christmas beetle crawled onto my foot. Sleeping on the ground began to look uninviting. These diamonds of men came to our rescue and brought over a wire shearer's stretcher, whereon together the children and I slept easy. The snake bite victim recovered with no ill effects.

Father Anthony Piele resided at Balgo for some years. A linguist, he wrote down the Gugadja language which was, until then, an unwritten language. He was often to be seen squatting on his heel at the camps of the old people, laughing and joking with them. He recorded many of the native plants and herbs, noting their native names and medicinal value. Without Fr. Piele's work, much of this knowledge would have been lost. Only in recent times is the wider population appreciating the benefits of the old herbs and medicines. A big fellow in baggy kakhi trousers, a shock of brown hair over childlike eyes. He called in at Bora for a couple of days some years later, when we had settled there. He was on his way from Balgo across the Top End to the East in his rough short wheel base four wheel drive. We did not know then he had not long to live.

It was well understood by all of us whites at Balgo that language is integral to a people's culture. "Language is the root of a culture. Take that away and a people have lost something forever," Father Mac reminded us. Though school was taught in English and the children bi-lingual, their mother language was respected. It is sad I think, to note that many indigenous children today are not fluent in English, and have fallen backward in the school arena, when education is so essential. I guess the "absolute rule" in our day had its benefits, in that, those desert children did learn to read and write.

Anthropologists were attracted to Balgo, because most of the people were not far from their age old nomadic way of life. Professor and Mrs. Berndt were among those who came to add to their learned studies of indigenous peoples, sitting in the camp talking to the 'old people'. The Berndts were no longer young, yet travelled great distances to remote locations way before air-conditioned cars. Looking back, I feel I largely took for granted those people we chanced to meet and with whom we shared some time.

David and Maree Heath with their two children, and Harry, the single teacher, came when the Lee's and Mark's two years were up. They were soon integrated into our little community, taking part in outings, exploring The Pound and rock holes, swimming or weekend trips out to the station, as well as teaching school. From Balgo, the Heath family went to the Cocos Islands, half way between Perth and Ceylon (Sri Lanka). David was selected by John Clunies Ross as advisory teacher for the Malay population.

Cocos as described in a letter from Maree in 1973 had a well organized community of Malays, with coconuts being their main industry. QANTAS and South African Airways also used an airstrip there, flying between South Africa and Australia. The Clunies Ross family had benevolently ruled the island group since 1827 when John Clunies Ross had made the first permanent settlement on the far flung coral atoll.

* * * * *

Bushfires and other Hazards

The men were out at Moody's bore fencing when we received a message from John, that they needed some gear out there. I was at the Mission. Brother Wally was to take the materials out and John had suggested the children and I go too. Pleased at the prospect, I rolled swags, packed extra rations and arranged for our poddy calf to be looked after.

With load on, Brother Wally, my kids and I, together with some mission kids, took off on an old track, not knowing there had been fires along it. With the spinifex burned, there was nothing to hold the sand back from the track. Time and again we bogged, then packed the scant spinifex under the tyres, churned along a bit and were bogged again. Eventually we gave up and camped.

Sometime through the night, the sound of a vehicle thrummed in the still desert air, its approach could be heard long before it arrived, with John at the wheel. In the headlights he summed up the situation. "Did you have it in second gear, low? And you have to keep going - don't stop!"
"We hadn't intended to stop, the wheels just refused to keep moving forward" I thought.

All I needed was a bed to drop into, preferably with someone to bring me a cup of hot tea. Dream on, Norah! At any rate I could always rely on my husband to do the practical thing, and that was a reassuring quality in hard country. He used the idea of letting our tyres down till they were almost flat, then with a bit of help, able to drive out. On we trundled, children sprawled asleep all over us.

Another trick I learned about dry bogs, was that the hard red termite nests were very effective if you could push them over and pack them under the tyres. They gave purchase to drive forward. Hot sand, during the day, may be impossible to drive through, but when it cools down at night, it packs harder and you can drive out of a bog. Bog mats were usually carried on our trucks. These were perforated steel, used by the army to lay temporary air strips.

Bushfires were a natural hazard. At the end of the dry season when storms built up in the heat, chain lightning streaking across the sky flickering angrily on the horizon could ignite the grass – dry as tinder – in a flash. Resinous spinifex burned fiercely, creating its own crackling atmosphere, black smoke billowing. A frightening sight with a wind behind it, only to be stopped when the wind changed and it burned back, thus extinguishing itself. At night the spectacular glow of a fire could be seen for many miles.

The stockmen deliberately lit fires so they could pick up some bush tucker, lizards and other delicacies. On the burnt country fresh green spinifex would spring up after rain; this was more palatable than the hard old tussocks. So this checkerboard effect over the country didn't matter too much. On hot days, whirlywinds spiralled darkly skywards from freshly burned areas.

One time while moving cattle, we packed the stock camp truck to move on to dinner camp. Bob, one of the stockmen, was driving, the bigger children on the back when we saw a fire burning ahead. It was on one side of the track so we dashed past it. Unfortunately there was a fair sized sand hill ahead, and on this we got stuck. We spent some anxious moments as we furiously tried to dig our way out. Meanwhile the fire had jumped the track and was getting ahead of us. Frantically working, I was mentally planning to drag the woollen blankets from swags to wrap the boys in, wool being almost impossible to burn. Thank God! Bob just got the vehicle inching along and over the worst. From there it was downhill, on we went to set up dinner camp.

Even now I get butterflies in my tummy at the sight of smoke on the horizon.

Cathedral Landscape

Going East

The time came when we thought of going East and securing a station manager's job, a little less remote. Arriving in Sydney, we left the children in the care of aunties, while John and I, nine months pregnant, traipsed around Sydney offices of pastoral firms. John gave his credentials to suited managers, sitting behind vast desks in high rise buildings. "John can handle most things. Nothing could be tougher or more demanding of a resourceful man than where we have been." That is what I felt. But we did not instantly have manager's jobs thrust at us.

While we were exploring our options in N.S.W. our fourth son, Conor, was born in Warren, hometown of my youth. We only just made it to town for his birth. Was it a sign of things to come? Even today Conor does things wholeheartedly and in a rush. At the time the Irish journalist, Conor Cruise O'Brien, was reporting events from the Congo. I loved the name, and of course, the legendary King Conor Mac Nessor of Ireland sounded pretty grand, so our baby was christened *Conor*.

John was asked if we would go back to Balgo. We didn't require much persuading. Life there was all absorbing, a rare experience. We headed west once more.

Father McGuire was transferred from Balgo after ten years. Given leave he travelled the world. Before me is an air letter from Tanzania in Africa illustrated with animals:

Dear Boys and Mum and Dad,

I hope you like all the animals on this letter, I have seen them all as well as lions, giraffes, elephants and other ones. Some day one of you might come to Africa as a missionary and so see them yourself. I hope Sean that you and Matthew are still learning the stock work and helping the stock-boys do things properly."

He was missing Balgo, declaring that he didn't have to recall stock, paddocks bores or bore sites, they were ever present with him. *"Naturally I would have liked to work alongside you both until we had it fully developed by 1980 but I must accept things as they are. I always appreciated your dedication and drive and we had no trouble developing each other's plans."*

Further on, these poignant words, *"I admit I badly need a long break to enable me to break the developed habit of making everyone sociable over a drink, in the early days such a practice was a necessity to build up friendships and hold labour in lonely places."*

Father Ray Hevern was appointed administrator, a formidable job for a goodhearted young priest from Melbourne.

Wings over the Spinifex

The wire (telegram) with the news of Dad's accident in N.S.W. arrived on the morning schedule at Balgo. My 77-year-old father, while making some routine adjustment on his car with the engine running, was run over. Somehow it had jumped into gear, pinning Dad, breaking ribs, puncturing his lung and inflicting multiple injuries. My mother and siblings had hastened to Sydney where he had been taken by air ambulance. My sister Claire was on her way from the South Solomons.

It was arranged that Bill Keene, the bishop's pilot, would fly me and our four small boys to Alice Springs to catch a commercial plane. Night was upon us when we landed at Mascot. My lovely brother and sisters met us on the tarmac, the children lovingly gathered up as we descended the steps of the plane. I had held myself together throughout the day's traveling - I needed to, with the children. I did not know what the news would be at journey's end. Dad was still alive! That's when the floodgates opened – it was inconceivable for me that Dad would die. Even to see our father in a hospital bed was shocking; he had hardly ever been sick.

Together with various siblings, the children and I stayed with Nan and John Waterford, our Kersh grandma and aunts stepping in to look after my crew when I visited the hospital. A fraught time followed as Dad hovered between life and death in intensive care. We, his family, kept vigil at the hospital.

Though overshadowed by concern, it was great to be together with my family.

Dad did recover. At first on crutches, he regained his strength, making light of his own ills. During his convalescence he was encouraged by Norma to write down some of his memories. The first part was written in an exercise book with his left hand, his right hand being out of commission. These notes became the genesis of a family history, *An O'Brien Odyssey,* written by my sister Fran.

Dad on the mend, it was time to go back home to John, and Balgo. Our return trip began by boarding a plane in the cool of early morning Sydney. We changed planes at Melbourne. A hostess appeared from nowhere to help me with the children - unbeknown to me Nan had arranged this. We then flew on to Adelaide and north to Alice Springs. The heat struck us as we landed with the full force of a February sun. I descended the steps to the searing tarmac, tired little boys asking for a drink. Tepid water dripped from a nearby tap as I filled paper cups.

Bishop Jobst of Broome, was at the airport to meet us in his light aircraft. Then followed the longest leg of our journey – three and a half hours over the Tanami and into the Great Sandy Desert. As we taxied, heat waves shimmered on the pink and mauve hills of the McDonnell Ranges. Wisps of cloud like angels' wings stream past. Six thousand feet up and levelling off, the bishop commented that he had rarely struck the air so turbulent. More cloud, thicker, more like storm clouds. "We need to get up higher" said the bishop.

Conor, sleeping in my arms was getting heavy, not much room. We were going up some more. "Better to dodge these updrafts and rough weather," reported the bishop. We rose to nine thousand feet. My brother Mike, a pilot, has told me that above ten thousand feet the air is so thin you can get short of oxygen, but you don't know it is happening, as a dangerous feeling of wellbeing overtakes you.

Did the bishop think I was the calm, confident type? Perhaps – on the exterior – but my fertile imagination tends to fly to worst-case scenarios. I began, right away, looking for likely landing spots, but had seldom seen anything so dry and desolate. Consoling myself, I was thinking "at least the bishop knows the route well," but with a jolt realized it was his pilot, Bill Keene, who usually did this flight. The children were all sleeping – we were flying high to keep above the clouds which were rapidly thickening.

"A little knowledge is a dangerous thing" they say. My little knowledge was that high up, the air is thin. Was the pilot's yawning a sign of imminent sleep? Not really – there was little chance of sleep for the bishop, the way he had to hold the aircraft controls to keep it balanced along the way. I watched the aerial map (spread in front) to follow our course, noting landmarks, so that when we were about the West Australian border (unmarked by a fence) I knew we were far south of where we should have been. We should have flown practically over Carroll's bore, or the homestead. Instead we were over myriad dry salt lakes, which I knew were down to the south. To make matters worse, there began to be showers of rain falling out of storm clouds. When dodging storms a pilot must calculate the degrees and time he changes course, then come back the same amount to keep on track. This can keep him busy in rough weather.

When the bishop took his rosary beads from his pocket, "Hail Mary full of grace" I didn't know whether to laugh or cry (me of little faith!). To my relief, he turned the craft north, I think to dodge the storms - or was he inspired? We flew over the legendary dry lakes but 'nary a one did I recognise until far out to our east, I espied a creek. I asked the bishop if he thought it was part of Kersh Springs. He asked me "Would you know it?" We flew towards it, going down lower. I was wondering if I could reliably distinguish it from the air. Lo and behold, it was quite recognizable - and then I spotted a fence line, then a track. Totally relieved, from there on in the last hundred miles, I more or less knew the lay of the land, its ranges all in the right place.

John was there to meet us as we came in over the beautiful pound country, its ironstone silver after a shower of rain. Relief is too mild a word. To be on solid ground – home. Little boys tumbled out of the aircraft into John's waiting arms. Conor nestled against me with not a care in the world, and my smart new suit was now clinging damply to my skin. I stepped down, my legs like jelly. Was it only that morning we had left a cool mist in Sydney?

Writing this now, I think of the extreme generosity of the bishop making his plane available for us when a crisis occurred. It is a long, long way from Alice Springs to Broome, where he lived.

No Room for Luxury Items - Life in the Stock Camp

Long before the eastern sky was pale, the horse tailer was on the job. He wakened listening for the intermittent soft clang of horse bells indicating where the working horses were feeding. As the rest of the stockmen were crawling from their swags and pulling on boots the horses were returning to camp; a quick breakfast with pannicans of sweetened black tea, the stockmen walked in among the milling horses, bridle in hand, to select the horse they would use that day. Hobbles were hung on the greenhide neckstrap, horses saddled and they were ready for the day's muster.

My day had begun earlier. Coaxing the fire into life being the first task, hanging the big billycans over it and slicing yesterday's bread to spread with jam from the four gallon tin. Our staple diet was beef and bread. Perhaps custard made from powdered milk and custard powder with dried apricots at night to accompany the main meal. These came by the carton in our six monthly orders from Perth, by ship to Derby or Wyndham. As all our gear had to fit on the current stock vehicle, swags, saddles, tucker box, medical kit as well as fuel and water drums, there was no room for luxury items.

Washing up out of the way, it was time to start the bread. Tinned dry-balm yeast was mixed in warm water; then I measured out a quantity of plain flour into a large tin dish. 18 kilogram flour drums were a vast improvement on bagged flour, which at the end of 6 months was riddled with weevils. Bread was covered and left to rise (before kneading and placing in the bread oven). There was washing to be done. If camped at a bore, I would put one bucket on the fire to heat, then carry it to the stock trough along with my tin dish, nappies and other clothes, get cold water from the trough and proceed with the job. Clumps of spinifex were perfect on which to spread nappies to dry - the spiny resilient desert grass both holding the cloth in place and allowing air all around. In the same way I cooled new-made bread. With a shovel scattering ashes and coals off the lid of the bread oven I could lift the lid with number 8 wire-hooks and tip the circular loaf out onto a clump of spinifex.

When we were running short of beef, the men covered the back of the truck with branches to lay the beef on, drove out to shoot and skin the beast, expertly butchering it into proper cuts – steak, roasts and so on. It was loaded on the back of the truck and brought back to camp. Fresh meat was cause for celebration, fried rib bones a favourite on the menu that night. The aboriginal stockmen didn't waste anything. Scooping up all the unmentionable parts we whites disdained, they threw them on the ashes, scarcely singeing them before beginning the feast. We would relish fresh roast and steak for a couple of days. In the absence of refrigeration, all the rest was slashed with sharp knives and coarse salt rubbed well in to preserve it. We then bagged it to hang in the shade by day and took it out by night to air, till it was thoroughly dried out. To re-constitute this, I soaked it before cooking as corned meat to be used hot or cold, or chopped up for a curry.

Because inland Australia has long summers we hear more about scalding weather. The cold comes as a shock to systems acclimatized to heat. At Balgo, when wind blew, it was staggeringly fierce. It had not much to slow it down, no big mountain ranges and trees - it made its wild passage on cloudless winter days. First hint of it early before daylight, it blew like crazy till about mid morning, then as suddenly stopped.

Our little boys just fitted into the routine, such as it was, of the stock-camp, taking an interest in their surroundings and creating games with imagination and whatever was at hand, as children do. Games revolved around the world they saw: "Come on Matt," Sean would suggest "You hold Brendan on me, and I'll be the bucking bull," at which Matt would pick up Brendan, nearly as big as himself, putting him on his brother's back, as Sean on all fours began tossing around. Or sitting in the shade of the tank near the cattle trough: "This is my place Sean," indicating a little fortress of mud. "I am making a track over to Pussycat Bore," dragging muddy fingers in a line. Sean is busy collecting a bundle of twigs and sticking them in the dirt: "I am making the branding yard, and I am Dad." They learned from the stockmen, could track various little desert creatures and spoke of snakes as either quiet or cheeky ones – the latter being poison and avoided at all costs.

One evening, when first settling cattle at Carroll's Bore, the men rode in excitedly discussing a spring they had discovered. We all piled onto the vehicle next day and made our way out there, scrub bashing through low desert eucalypt, bumping our way over spinifex till our bones rattled. Then, among a tangle of scrub and snappy gums, we saw the spring with a trickle of water running along a washed-out gully. Suddenly the grey green of bush fell away. An escarpment extending in a vast semi-circle stretched as far as the eye could see. We were gazing across a salt lake. A silver ribbon of water meandered its way across the white glare of salt, diminishing in flickering mirage, hurting our eyes with its brightness. Father MacGuire named this place Kersh Spring, as was his custom of naming bores and other landmarks after people who worked at Balgo. Did it have a native name? I don't know. These Balgo stockmen didn't know of it, but deaf Dominic when he came out was excited and showed us, with motions of rocking a baby in his arms, that he had been here when he was a picaninni.

*   *   *   *   *

Cattle Rush

Carroll's Bore was a central camp for us as the cattle muster proceeded. Once again I was camp cook. John and the boys had erected a sturdy bough shed next to a couple of bloodwood trees. Carroll's bore water was sweet, the Comet windmill clanking a homely tune as it turned in the wind, replenishing water in tanks and troughs. Around this set up was a holding paddock.

Jack Carroll was an old station saddler, white haired, staunch friend of Father MacGuire. Carroll's Bore was named for him. When Brendan was born, our baby stroller with steel frame had a canvas seat much the worse for wear. Jack took it from me and returned it with a new saddle leather seat, stitched with a perfect saddler's stitch.

Carroll's is situated twenty odd miles south west of the station homestead. The track from the homestead took us south past Middleton's Lake. A dazzling expanse of shallow water after a wet, we pass the windmill and trough at the foot of a low range. Just a smudge of purple from the homestead, rough and rocky close up. Then the country opens out, a vast open plain liberally strewn with massive ant-hills eight or ten feet high. I named this place The Sea of Tranquility, a moonscape. The first moon landing was a recent event. Crossing the plain a line of grey green appears in the distance, mulga country, thence on to Carroll's.

In fact Carroll's became like a home to us as we spent more time there. I had collected ant beds – the hard spire shaped red termite nests, and placed them in a semi-circle around the fire place, partly as a wind-break, partly to make an area into a home. Sean and Matt paddled happily in the overflow at the bore to cool off. I did the washing by the trough and spread Brendan's nappies and clothes on clumps of spinifex to dry.

About 80 yards from the tanks and troughs, we parked the stock camp truck alongside the bough shed, with assorted necessities – tucker box, buckets, billies, saddles nearby- and hung bagged salted meat from the bloodwood tree.

The campfires burned down to glowing coals - married men's fire, single men's fire and whitefella's fire - each surrounded by sleeping bodies in their swags, and the saddled night-horses, heads drooping under a tree. This was the nightly scene when moving cattle.

Stockmen took turns riding round the cattle keeping them settled from sundown till sun up. Taking two-hour watches, the less experienced stockmen took early watches turning the odd restless animal back in as it wandered off feeding. When the whole mob was settled down sleeping, any unexpected sound - a snapping stick as a horse walked on it, a dingo howling, or a cough - could startle the mob into instant panic. The cattle would be on their feet rushing, taking no account of what was in their path. This is why the night watcher must constantly make a noise. So he sang, it didn't matter what, just the lulling sound of his voice to keep the mob calm and disguise anything out of the ordinary.

One night, I remember, as we camped with our travelling mob, I heard one of our stockmen singing - in his own Gugadga language, but the tune was that of "The Carnival is Over", a popular song of the Seekers at the time. Quite lovely to my ear as I gazed at a million stars above and contemplated the ageless Sandy Desert around us.

Evenings were beautiful, I thought. Day's work was done, children bathed and changed into sun-dried clothes. Supper over, dark figures merged into shadow arranging swags around fires, young men chiacking one another. Old men's voices speaking Gugadja, their muffled tones ending in long drawn out syllables. Pungent tang of cattle camp mingled with drifts of dust as night horses stamped, jingling bits and creaking leather. The hoot of a night bird echos among silvered mulga branches. Peaceful sounds really. The last pannican of tea is finished and tapped out on the tucker box. "Another good day," I think as I check the row of enamel plates draining on the tea chest. I snuggle into the swag beside John and behold the heavens sprinkled with stars "Who would want to be anywhere else in the world?" I ponder sleepily.

On an ordinary night during mustering, a good sized mob of cattle were in the holding paddock ready to be handled next day. We were asleep in the middle of the night when suddenly, all was chaos. With a thunder of hooves, five hundred cattle were up and rushing, bellowing in fear. A terrifying sound. Enveloped in darkness, pounding of hooves shook the earth. I could hear shouts and branches snapping like rifle shots. It was impossible to tell in these seconds just where the mob was. I could hardly breathe, for dust, noise and sheer fright. My thoughts were for the children as I snatched them up and scrambled into the truck. Tousled and sleepy, they knew not the danger as the mob tore past amidst grit and dust. The pure panic of the cattle transmitted to me: a mother's instinct working on automatic. The worst was over quite soon – the mob had flattened the fence of the holding paddock and scattered into the night, their pitiful frightened bellowing echoing in the distance.

Well! There was no one as good as those Aboriginal stockmen for making the most of a situation. It wasn't long before the fires were blazing up and men ringed around recounting their close shave. In fact, the worst injuries were scratches inflicted as they fled. Billies and pannicans were scattered, mulga broken and smashed. The drama was re-enacted over and over as the weeks went on.

After that, my first experience of a rush, I have had a healthy respect for camped cattle, yarded up, or on an open camp. Cattle at night can be easily spooked. Drovers stories of rushes are legion.

She Won't Make it

Would this road never end? It was long enough in daylight, but at night, torturous. Negotiating rugged dry creeks through the gap at Lorna Springs, turning this way and that to avoid getting hung up on a washout, the driver had to keep his wits about him. Crawling through particularly sandy places, keeping the revs just right not to stall, but not too fast thus making the wheels spin, and dry bog. It was all par for the course.

For the past week I had been worrying with a threatened miscarriage – my fifth pregnancy, the year 1971. Over the radio I had sought advice. "You must rest," said the doctor. "More easily said than done." I thought, but did my best. The little ones were all over me, not understanding about rest.

The stock camp was out. Our old friend, John Honner, was at the homestead, along with two Aboriginal women and their toddlers (families of the stockmen) as well as Sean, Matt, Brendan and Conor. I tried to rest but my condition was unchanged. John came home from camp to drive me to the mission, so we were on the way; I was haemorrhaging badly. When at some unearthly hour we arrived, John roused Fr. Mac, then Sr. Francis. The special whistle was used on the radio to activate the flying doctor base. It was arranged that a plane would be on its way at first light.

Dick Robertson, a WWII pilot, had a push-pull six-seater aircraft that was called upon when necessary. The back seats were pulled out to make room for a stretcher. Dick arrived at dawn with a nurse to care for me. I felt as weak as a kitten and for the first time in my life, fainted, crossing the hospital verandah on my way to the plane. It surprised me to wake up on the plane. We taxied and took off in the direction of Derby, five hundred miles away.

Flying along, feeling quite peaceful, I heard the nurse who was monitoring me say to the pilot "We will have to divert to Halls Creek. She won't make it to Derby". I was not meant to hear this, I feel sure. So now Dick began calling on his radio trying to contact the little Australian Inland Mission hospital in Halls Creek which was run by two gallant young nurses. These girls had to contend with any kind of emergency which arose, doctors being hundreds of miles away. Contact was made asking for them to come out to the airstrip with plasma to sustain me, the patient, because of blood loss. Duly our light aircraft banked over the little town of Halls Creek and taxied along the airstrip, just as the dust settled around the hospital vehicle coming to a stop.

Efficiently the two young women brought their equipment to transfuse me. They were to insert the needle into a vein in my arm and let the plasma run in. Try as they might, the veins were too flat, so they tried my legs but with the same outcome. They were unable to get a vein. The poor girls tried to keep the anxiety out of their voices; I realised they had failed in their efforts.

I thought then that I would die. We had taken time to divert, all to no avail – Derby was a long way away. It seemed a shame – John, my parents, siblings would be so sad. I was not frightened myself. Too tired. But my children! I could not bear to leave them. I never did – they needed me. But here I was wafting off, too drained to worry.

And - here I am, many years later. It was not my time. Somewhere on the flight to Derby I recall the nurse saying I had stabilised. The ambulance was at the airport to take me to the hospital. I had lost my baby.

It was during the week in hospital I met up with Noel Dobbin, in with a bout of hepatitis. He was our Halls Creek stock inspector. Later we travelled back on the mail plane via Wyndham, where we had lunch, then on to Halls Creek, where Noel and his young wife, Toni, took me to their home. That night Bro. Michael picked me up in the semi-trailer as he returned from Wyndham with a load. We travelled through the night the one sixty miles home, with the cab of the truck having few of the modern day comforts.

The doctor in Derby had told me that future pregnancies could be risky, but two years later Kimberley came along. I was in hospital with him in Young when news that Gough Whitlam had been elected Prime Minister was announced. Excitement rippled through the Mercy hospital. Change was at hand.

Collecting the four boys from my relatives, and with two week old Kimberley, we flew once more via Adelaide to Alice Springs from Sydney. John met us at Alice Springs where he and men had finished loading the mission semi, which was to travel with us. We had the Toyota, and set off that same evening. As was our practice, we left town to put a few miles behind us (about eighty) before making camp. The four older boys shared a swag with little covering required, it was so hot. I constantly wiped Kim's little body with a wet washer to keep him from dehydrating. Fortunately he breastfed well and did not stress.

A memorable incident occurred that night. We saw lights approaching, rare enough as few travelled that road. The normal thing would be for the occupants, whoever they were, to stop and exchange news and maybe share a billy of tea. As we sat up, the sudden crack of two sharp rifle shots split the night air. Perhaps a quarter of a mile off, but far too close for comfort. "What the heck!" John dashed to our vehicle, switching on the lights, blinking them rapidly to indicate our presence. With that, the strangers gunned their motor and charged past in a shower of gravel and dirt - and were gone, red tail lights wobbling into the distance. We never got to speak to those people, but decided they had been out getting themselves some fresh beef - obviously not their own. We had disturbed them with our unexpected appearance and sent them packing.

A cradle made from packing cases in Old Mission days, by one of the brothers, was Kimberley's cradle. It was styled lovingly with cross legs as on a Christmas card, with a little heart carved at the head. I had painted it with enamel paint and added a few daisies for decoration.

Grandma O'Brien, Dad's mother, whose descendants were numerous, unfailingly sent a gift of a dozen white nappies to each new great-grandchild. A welcome gift. They must have been of the best quality; ours were passed down till they flapped on the clothes line threadbare, but intact. Clothing needs for the children were simple. The mission was the recipient of bales of charity clothes; I found old fashioned garments with plenty of material and re-hashed them into little shirts and shorts. Checks, stripes and spots were stitched together in harmonious abandon, with my Singer sewing machine.

Social Event of the Year

The scattered population of the immense North West seemed to make little impact on this part of the continent, almost unchanged over the millenniam as it absorbed torrential rains of the "Wet" and scorching winds of the "Dry". Because we were so scattered, getting together took on grand proportions. The races were the social event of our year. Kimberley stations had well bred horses as all stock work was done on them. Leading up to the races, those chosen as the best gallopers had to be taken to the one paddock so they would have an equal "grass fed" chance.

The Negri races were held on Nicholson, one of the Vestey stations, which extended from Wave Hill in the Northern Territory across into the East Kimberley. I think Inverway, owned by the Underwood family, was the only non-Vestey property across that vast tract of land.

Preparations for the annual races went into gear well before the event. Large flour bags were unpicked and sewn to make walls around our temporary shelters, cooking buckets and utensils, medical kits, swags, vehicles, water drums, spare tires, fan belts – the lot, were readied for the two hundred-mile trek to the Linacre racetrack. Amid much hilarity, the Balgo population climbed into the stock crates on the Commer trucks – children, personal effects, billies, and swags all somehow finding a place.

Our family travelled by Landrover, the two youngest children in the cab with John and me, the others on the back with a few of the stockmen - plus swags, water and fuel drums. Much thought had gone into organizing for the trip and races. "Good clothes" were packed for the four-day event - which entailed two days of racing and two days of rodeo. In went the medical kit, with everything from stitches in case of accident, to the bottle of Kaomagma for "guts ache". I feared this common ailment for our usually (thank God) healthy lot. It was dreadful to see these energetic little boys laid low, limp and lacklustre with diarrhea. Dangerous for small children so easily dehydrated in often soaring temperatures. That was when I felt the isolation - hundreds of miles from a doctor.

A particularly treacherous sand hill between the mission and Sturt Creek station required the mission grader to tow the trucks over. Everyone disembarked and collectively held their breath as it was negotiated, churning along inch by inch in the fine red sand - letting out a cheer when the top was reached. We made our way from Sturt Creek north through the Mitchell grass country of Gordon Downs and on to Nicholson.

Arriving at our destination, each station set up camps in a radius back from the graded race track. These had to be prepared prior to the event. Our camp was a collection of bough sheds, the local snappy gums providing the uprights. Stitched bags hung for walls and windbreaks. A shower with overhead tank was the height of luxury after the warm dusty days. A bush table in the dining area was near the fire place, the main centre of activity. Two of the Balgo Sisters, in white habits, were always busy cooking, presiding over the mission girls, combing their hair or generally keeping an eye on things.

If days were full, night life was equally so. Len and Robyn Hill from Nicholson as host station, threw a party each year at their well-appointed camp. Conversation flowed as we caught up with friends and met new ones. Under starry skies romances bloomed, silhouetted bauhinias increasing the beauty of the night as smoke from campfires drifted heavenwards.

Old friends come to mind. Thea and Ralph Hayes were at Gordon Downs when we first met. They had three little sons and later a beautiful daughter. I will include a story about Ralph here.

During the war, his parents were on Waterloo Station, N.T. The time came for his mother "Cudge" to have her second baby. The trip to Wyndham was arduous, the climate hot and steamy, so it was decided that toddler Ralph would remain on the station with his father and with the help of the Aboriginal house girls. Bereaved, Ralph fretted so much for his mother that he stopped eating. In Ralph's words "I was a scrawny little kid at the best of times". Seeing the little fellow pining away, one of the Aboriginal women, Murrawah, put him to her breast to comfort him. Though she had no children of her own, nature prevailed. She made milk and breastfed him. From then on, Ralph began to thrive.

Years later the Hayes family was together again on Limbunya station, when Murrawah got word that they were there and turned up in the camp. She ambled up to the kitchen to talk to the "missus", greeting Cudge with "I bin come to see my boy Ralph". Taken aback, Cudge replied "Come on Murrawah! You know Ralph is my son".
"You might be make 'im, but I bin grow 'im up" Murrawah flashed back.

No wonder, as an adult running one of the biggest cattle stations in Australia, Ralph had a capacity beyond others to work with Aboriginal people. He spoke their native language he'd learned at the breast. He had respect for the "Old People" as he called them.

Thea, Ralph's wife, had come from Wollongong to nurse at Wave Hill when Ralph was head stockman. Heads turned when she alighted from the plane. They say the young ringers were falling over themselves to get to the infirmary with some concocted ailment.

Around that fire at Nicholson camp I recall Dorothy, a friend of Thea's, who had come north to nurse. She met and married Sabu Peter Sing who had grown up with Ralph around the stations. A noted horseman in a land of horsemen, he and Dorothy had a family and contract mustered in that rugged country of big rivers. Sabu was tragically killed in a car accident. A handsome bronze statue of Sabu on horseback stands in Katherine, honouring all stockmen.

For the Aboriginal population, who had their own separate social life, the races were a meeting time with relations from other places. In the sixties there still prevailed the complex skin system of relationships. Who could 'look at' whom and who could not. Complicated for whites but instantly understood by aboriginal people. For example, a vehicle from hundreds of miles away might rock up to the mission, aboriginal visitors jump off and amidst shaking of hands and slapping of backs, it was soon established who was whose cousin, uncle or aunt even though they had never seen each other before.

The Mission was in a delicate position of balancing old ways with the new, respecting old laws but unable to support some of them. Teenagers were rebelling against old custom, where girls could be promised to old men who may already have a Number 1 and Number 2 wife. Father Mac in some cases was able to negotiate a deal with the old man to allow the girl her freedom. So the young people with whom the Sisters worked were, especially at races time, quite a responsibility.

The Ord River people put on a corroboree at Balgo camp. Dark shapes lit up as painted bodies crouched and leapt to tapping of clapping sticks and chant. Flat feet hammered the ground faster and faster, the sound rising to a crescendo, dust and smoke blurring wild movement. All the while the thrumming drone of didgeridoo rose and fell, so deeply part of that country. I sat among the outer circle of white people in the frayed edges of firelight. Corroboree came to an end when Father Mac thought it was becoming too graphic for our delicate eyes!

At the race course, the hawker's truck was part of the set up. Overflowing with new shirts, hats, dresses, boots and belts it was patronized by whites and blacks alike. Pay cheques used up on new and tempting goods. Bright shirts of red or black satin with white piping were worn with flair, dark skins setting them off. They frequently changed hands, gambled over a game of cards.

A ball was held in the corrugated shed to conclude celebrations. It was not to be missed. We women took care with dress for these affairs. Weeks before the races, I had studied the mail order catalogue from Boans of Perth for a dress, or material with which to construct one. Wendy Lee, the Balgo schoolteacher, and I had combed the mission charity boxes searching for something suitably exotic for the novelty night with the theme, *Arabian Nights*. The latest hair styles seem to have filtered through to this remote spot. Long hair was the norm as there was no hairdresser within reach. The amazing bee-hive hair-do appeared and smoky mascaraed eyes with pale lips "the look". Gorgeous velvet hot pants with boots stole the show in the fashion stakes one night.

Race days had the movement and colour of more famous race venues. Horses gleamed as they were led to the saddling paddock, jockeys mounted, and then it was out into the straight. Champing at the bit they cantered round to the starting point. Spectators jostled to place bets before lining the rail – a row of lean, hatted figures – cut-outs against a backdrop of blue sky and bleached grass, extending into distant wavering mirage. Excitement mounted as horses took off, a whirl of dust spiralling out behind. Even the children drawn from their games ran up to watch as the field clattered past the winning post – the "Ladies Bracelet" had been decided for another year.

The bar in that thirsty climate always drew a crowd, some times erupting into a fight when some over-exuberant character got out of hand. Fighters were corralled by the police and locked in a stock crate, secured with weld mesh over the top. When the grog wore off, sore-headed and sorry they were allowed back on the social scene.

In spite of late nights, dawn would see ringers on the job bringing cattle up for the bullock rides, or exercising their favourite horses. Early morning sun's rays cast long shadows of women already busy over fires cooking quantities of steak, and children scrambling from swags to greet the brand new day.

Homecoming

After nearly seven years we made the decision to leave Balgo. My brother Miceal had bought a property near Quambone and portion of Yahgunyah. John and I were offered the other portion, which included the homestead. My parents by this time had moved to Warren.

John and I had agonized over the decision. Balgo had become so much part of us and we of it, I felt. An isolated life but rewarding. Considering school: Correspondence was alright, I had started Sean and Matt. But, what of the future? Boarding schools were two thousand and more miles distant. That did not appeal. Also, when and if we left, we wanted to be able to put heart and soul into any new venture, as we had at Balgo, while youth was on our side.

Now we were packing our belongings into a big crate to go on the mission truck to Alice Springs, thence by train south to Adelaide and east. Mahoods, when leaving Mongrel Downs for their own cattle place in Queensland had given our kids some toys including a beautifully constructed miniature windmill. So frugal we were, I still regret not packing this masterpiece. We just took what we then considered necessities. I would do it differently now if I had the chance. "Man does not live by bread alone." The children were excited. They were accustomed to packing up for stock-camp, going to the Mission, going to get a 'killer', to meet the mail plane; 'Moving Camp' like this, to a new place in N.S.W. sounded like an adventure.

Our family had been at Balgo at the tail end of a period when the old ways for both tribal people and Kimberley station people in general, were changing. Balgo people who had come in from the desert and a completely tribal life, moving about in small family groups only to meet on ceremonial occasions, were witness to their children learning to read and write, to drive motor vehicles, herd cattle and play the guitar. Migration towards those frontier towns, where different clans sometimes clashed, had begun. Some unscrupulous whites were only too ready to profit by selling flagons of wine to those who had little understanding of money. An array of challenges had to be faced in these new and strange circumstances.

Before our departure a send off was held at the teacher's house at the Mission. Goodbye to a marvellous bunch of people as diverse as they come, yet all sharing a part of our lives in an extraordinary setting. Packed to the limit next morning tears were shed, stockmen, women and children crying for their "Bush babies" who were leaving. We, like others who had spent time with Aboriginal people had been given "skin" names linking us truly to Balgo and its people. John is Tjapangarti, and I am Nampitjin. Our sons are Tjapanangka and our daughters Napanangka, our daughters-in-law are Napurrula.

Keeping the kids happy on the long miles kept me occupied, trying to be enthusiastic pointing out landmarks, a plains turkey, asking riddles, as John avoided sand bogging all the way to the bitumen near Alice. Further on, at Tennant Creek, we indulged in a rare delight of ice creams all round. Unfamiliar to their diet, or was the milk sour in the heat? They were all sick before an hour had passed. We stopped to clean up, wash down, and air hastily rinsed bits of clothing which were hanging out windows as we took off again.

Air-conditioned cars were but a future dream.

It was a homecoming for me. Old neighbours around the district unchanged, childhood friends now with growing families of their own. For John a different challenge was presented: this was the first time we had land of our own. An irrigation scheme taking water from the Macquarie River into the Marthaguy Creek was on the drawing board. As the Marthaguy flowed through Yahgunyah, we were on the lower reaches of this scheme. John became quite involved. Instead of numbers of stockmen to organize, cattle and wind droughts* to contend with, he was doing the rounds of clearing sales, looking at second-hand tractors and ploughs. He was blasting out stumps of gum trees and stick-picking to clear an area for cultivation.

Living at Yahgunyah was balm to my soul. The excitement, the wonder and challenge of life at Balgo had sustained me. I had not realized it had taken its toll. The almost unconscious but ever present worry of something happening to one of the children, a scrap of diary reminds me: "Conor's cold improving, Brendan running a temperature, Matt on penicillin for coal burn" and often dealing with situations totally on one's own was tough. Now, with the children running around the verandah and tumbling on the lawn, or meeting Mike and Eb and their children for a muster and branding, a weight had lifted off me. Mike and Helen were on one boundary, our cousins on adjoining Mayfield and Glenanaar, with Margaret and Eb Hayden on Noonbah to the west. We were able to baby-

---

* *Wind drought: Without wind for a few days, windmills were as "still as painted ships upon a painted ocean", failing to pump up bore water into tanks and troughs for thirsty stock. When this happened, a stand-by pumpjack was started to mechanically pump the water. An essential task was "checking waters".*

sit for one another as required. At times we could meet and travel together. So much was taken for granted but so good and enjoyable.

Maureen, Philomena, Fran and Mike, on grazing or farming properties, and their families lived around the general area. So during the years at Yahgunyah we appreciated to the full visits to my siblings and their families, and got to know better our delightful nieces and nephews. It was somewhat closer too, for John's occasional visit to Sydney, or for his folk to visit us for a few days.

Helen had come from Sydney to marry Mike and in the course of time they had seven sons. Helen seemed afraid of nothing, and being outgoing was usually secretary of the Parents and Citizens, Red Cross or president of the local Agricultural Show. Preparing to help Mike one day with stock, she was thrown from her horse, breaking both wrists. Damien was a baby a few months old. Imagine the frustration of her situation! We helped each other as much as possible looking after children, though looking back, the days were so full I barely had time to contemplate just how difficult this time was for Helen.

Life sailed along. They were good days. Our little boys, when visiting the O'Briens, would sanctimoniously remind their cousins 'Visitors first' when chocolate cake was passed around at smoko. This scene was repeated by the little cousins when they visited us.

Quentin, Joe and Rosana were born into our family. Only a line here, though each one an epic. In Warren hospital I luxuriated in the chance to have a rest, having my beautiful baby brought to me at meal time bathed and wrapped in a cocoon of fluffy blanket, a halo of soft black hair round angelic face. Breakfast, dinner and tea carried in by a staff member who inevitably knew my family and relations. Time to write neglected letters and read books. Receiving visits from neighbours and friends in town for the day. A welcome break before the reality and bustle of the home front. A baby in the house brought out the best in everyone, no matter how tired or busy, just to look at that little person waving arms in the bassinet put a smile on the most serious face. Rosana's birth caused the district to throw hats in the air, in celebration of our first girl. Wonderous to have a daughter, and so lovely, a sister for the boys. Like the princess in the story "she was as good as she was beautiful."

The older children travelled by bus to the little school in Quambone. Popeye Wright patiently drove the bus along the main road picking up each group of station kids at their mail boxes. The oldest of the children drove the younger ones from home in vehicles of varying antiquity, leaving it at the mailbox till the return journey in the afternoon. It was only when they grew up we heard the hair-raising stories of feats they made their conveyances perform.

What a joy it was to have my parents just an hour's drive away! Inevitably a kettle on the stove for a cup of tea and a mulberry tree out the back for the boys to raid. Plus Grandad's shed, where he showed them how to make interesting things. In his old age Ned was asked by the headmaster at the convent school to teach the boys woodwork. A bush carpenter like many country men, he now had to learn the finer points. True to form, he went to the library and studied woodwork books in order to teach the school boys the intricacies of dovetail joints. I am presently sitting on one of his sturdy wooden stools. My mother had some leisure to enjoy some of her talents. Her sons-in-law sported her much sought after beautifully hand-spun hand-knitted woollen jumpers. She and Ned always had time for the many people, young and old, who dropped in. Norma's hands were rarely idle.

Going to Bora

With seven active boys, and nine month old baby girl, John began to cast his eyes towards bigger horizons. Contending with regulations and restrictions of irrigation farming in the Warren-Quambone district, he thought there would be greater opportunities for expansion further out. We began to look for another grazing property. I could see the sense and reasons for moving, but leaving Yahgunyah, neighbours and relations was a wrench. However I loved the outside country and was soon caught up in the excitement of the changes.

John and I inspected a property for sale in the Walgett area shortly before attending the Wool Cup races in Coonamble. There we met up with my cousin Bernard O'Brien and his wife, Carmel, who owned Burendah Stud near Auguthella.

"What! Looking round Walgett? What about Queensland? Great Mitchell grass country and it doesn't cost the world." Not a man to let the grass grow under his feet, inside a week Bernard was on the telephone to John with a list of places for sale.
'I am taking a load of rams to Winton. Could you meet me there?'

A great judge of country, Bernard's suggestion was too good an offer to pass up, so it was organized. John and Sean drove up the thousand miles and met Bernard in Winton.

Matt

Bora homestead, Bora creek from the air.

Bora in 'the dry' Brendan behind cattle.

Bora start of 'the wet' Zade is happy.

Sean's handiwork, Cathedral mailbox with kids.

John with Bernadette at Cathedral.

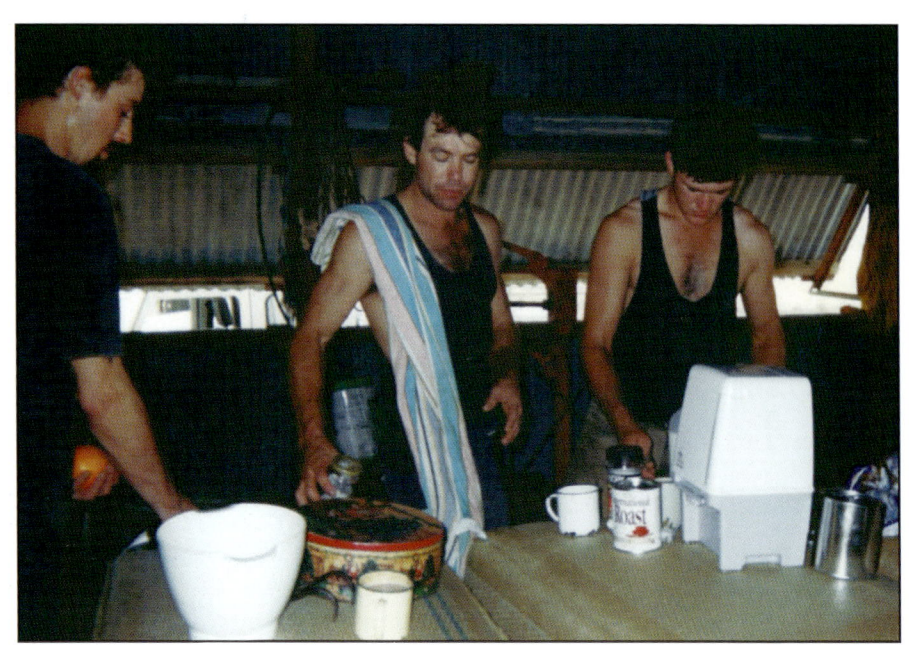

Smoko at Bora shearing shed, Scott, Matt and Quentin.

The boys calf branding.

Rosana and Bernadette display their artwork.

Sean and Bernadette.

Bernadette on her wedding day.

Kimberley bronco riding.

Kimberley with youngest daughter Violet.

Rosana.

Rosana and Mackenzie her niece.

Joe.

Joe cattle and Bora creek.

Quentin at
Runemede Rodeo.

Quentin.

Brothers.

146

It was October, 1978. There had been early storms and roads were impassable to all but four wheel drive vehicles. The Winton parish priest, a friend of Bernard's, insisted they take his four wheel drive to go out and inspect the properties. The pick of them in John's opinion was Akunam, belonging to Bucknells, near Corfield.

This was to be a "walk in walk out" sale, which meant to buy every thing as it was, including stock. On his return John tried to obtain a loan sufficient for the purchase. All in vain. The banks did not have our confidence and optimism. However now that the idea was planted and agents in the North West knew of us as prospective buyers, there was 'movement at the station'. Laurie Facer, stock and station agent from Richmond N.W. Qld., rang and told us of Bora - owned by Ernest and Naida Lord.

"If they are fair dinkum they can have a look" Ernest had told Laurie. In January '79 John Kersh, with my brother-in-law John Spora, and nephew Andrew Crawford flew up to Richmond with Bill Killen, a neighbour who had a light plane. Having full confidence in their ability to judge country, I was left holding the fort at Yahgunyah with the children. On their return a couple of days later, I had a hundred questions. "What was the kitchen like?"
"Good, quite big," was John's reply.
"The stove - what kind? Floor covering? What colour?"
"The kitchen? It did the job. Mrs. Lord gave us a good feed." My curiosity had to wait.
He added "Stockyards are solid, shearing shed and fences in good order, and the Mitchell grass is really something else!" John's voice grew enthusiastic.

Sean had been at Red Bend College in Forbes and sent a letter home, with a few instructions: "Good to hear about Bora, I hope it is a good place. The yards and dam and house look good. When the clearing sale is on if my filly does not make $450 can you keep her until the May holidays so that I can give her some work and get her going well. Make sure you don't sell the Barkoo saddles."

We bought Bora 'walk in walk out' with 8000 sheep for which we could wait till after shearing before paying. A beautiful station - open Mitchell grass downs country, well watered with several creeks junctioning on Bora and watered by two artesian bores. When buying a property, type of country and water is paramount; the house is usually of secondary importance. So what a bonus that Bora homestead, built by the Lords who had six daughters, was a large two-storey home. Electricity was supplied by the 240- volt generator which was cranked up each evening for lights; one became conscious of, and planned for chores requiring power when the generator was running. rather than thoughtlessly flicking a switch as I do today. We had kerosene fridges, fine-tuning required getting the wicks just right or they would sulkily exude black kero-smelling smoke.

We left Yahgunyah, shedding our winter woollies as we travelled north. John and older boys drove up in the truck with semi trailor, with much equipment plus dogs. My sister Nan had kindly offered to share the driving; we had the younger children and baby Rosana in the station wagon. We called in at Burendah near Augathella for lunch on the second day of travel. Bernard and Carmel O'Brien then owned this sheep stud. Carmel graciously served us lunch on Spode china with linen serviettes; I watched my travel-stained children seated around the polished table, on tenterhooks lest they knock a glass over, willing them to be on their best behavior.

We crossed the Tropic of Capricorn and reached Winton, where we picked up a new Suzuki. So for the last hundred miles we were a convoy of three vehicles. With nearly a thousand miles behind us, that last hundred seemed to me a long dirt road. The sun was sinking as we passed through the boundary gate, dipped into Rupert Creek and up across the paddock. High Mitchell grass either side of the track, over a couple more creeks, a grid, past the cattle yards - there the homestead lights were a happy sight.

The generator in the shed belted out its tune as we were greeted by Ernest and Naida Lord and daughter, Erica, home at the time. A beautiful girl, she showed us over the house and we found beds for our sleepy younger children. Naida was a Slack-Smith who had come up from N.S.W. with her family after the war. Slack-Smiths settled in the Nelia district; her brothers had walked a mob of horses up from Come By Chance. As so often happens, connections are found everywhere: Naida and her sister, Rahna, had been at boarding school in Coonamble with my sisters years before. Naida was now leaving the home where she had reared her family; nonetheless she had found time to bake a brownie for our cake tin, order a new batch of young chooks and had tomatoes coming into flower in the vegetable garden.

At the crack of dawn next morning our children were out exploring. They located the rubbish dump in the horse paddock and came running home excited – the treasures they had collected! No doubt this was stuff Naida had cleared out leaving the store room shelves clear for the new owners. Well! Conor had found a cracked china salt shaker, Quentin a toy with no wheels, someone else a gaudy vase with just one handle broken off – all were presented to me with love. How could I not re- install them in their home?

Neighbours around the district welcomed us – the new family at Bora. Our 'next door' neighbours at Plainby, fourteen miles distant, were the Batt Family with six grown children. The two teenage daughters told us later they had looked forward to the arrival of the Kersh's with seven sons; what a let down to discover that the eldest was only fourteen years of age!

There is an old story that tells of the stock and station agent inspecting a station for sale with his client. The client looks the place over then asks "What are the neighbours like?" "What are they like where you come from?" replies the agent. "They are great, we will be sorry to leave them – all good people." "You will find them much the same around here", assures the agent. The next inspection of the same place goes in a similar manner. The question is asked about the neighbours, "How do you find the neighbours down your way?" asks the agent. "Terrible," says the client "can't get on with them". The agent wryly states "You will find them much the same here".

Three years after we settled at Bora, Bernadette was born. Sean and Matt were at boarding school at Mt. Carmel in Charters Towers. I had gone down to stay with my sister Maureen and brother-in-law Bill Crawford at their property near Coonamble, to be closer to town. Even so, it was a fast night trip to town for Bernadette's birth. She had quite severe talipes, her poor little feet misshapen.

'They can be fixed, but she won't be a ballet dancer' announced the doctor bluntly. Maybe not a ballet dancer, but thanks to the wonderful surgery of Dr. Douglas in Townsville, her feet were rebuilt. When, at eighteen months, the final plasters came off her legs, she practically flew. Grant and Rita Lillyman from Kara in the basalt country north of Richmond, who have travelled much of the gravelled road of life with us since, agreed to be her godparents. Now as a nurse Bernadette, has worked as a volunteer in Kenya and is a fly-in fly-out nurse to a mine in north west Qld.

*　　　　*　　　　*　　　　*　　　　*

Areas of Blowing Dust

For two years we kept Lords' bullocks on agistment, until dry seasons struck. It was always a happy event when Ernest came to muster his cattle - sometimes with his daughter, Leigh, to help. Our bigger boys saddled up to join the fun. Once more, north of Capricorn on the edge of the Gulf country, here we were in the land of the 'Wet' and the 'Dry.' Seasons such as autumn with red and golden falling leaves or spring with blossoming trees do not exist.

It was rare to see a dew at Bora and even more rare to see a frost. Sometimes though when there was some moisture in the atmosphere it did happen. I took a photo of icicles dripping off the ladder on our tank-stand, the overflow from the tank having frozen overnight. Some trees in the garden died from cold that year.

The tank high on the steel tank-stand held our house supply pumped from the mill at the dam a quarter of a mile away. When the tank was low someone was delegated to go and turn the mill on. Pity help anyone leaving the hose on overnight and running the tank dry. It was both garden and washing water supply. Pristine white nappies and sheets assumed a slightly coffee tinge after a few washes, due to the dam water.* I got

---
* *An enterprising Hughenden mother began dyeing bore water stained nappies bright colours. She turned the idea into a popular commercial venture called Bright Bots.*

to love walking to turn on the windmill, especially at dusk as birds winged their way towards darkening creek lines, trees just scribbles against pearly sky. The long Dry of cloudless blue skies, green grass turning yellow, ground opening up in cracks, follows the more dramatic Wet season. Inland, as at Balgo, the short burst of winter can be very cold. Add to that the chill factor when riding a horse or bike. All too soon winter passes, September afternoons grow hot. Into October and November we watch the sky for signs of an early storm. Radio weather forecasts are a matter of interest. My imagination is captivated by some of the wording – "Areas of blowing dust or possible scattered storms elsewhere."

In a good season, when there is still a body of grass, dry storms are a real danger – the tinder dry grass ready to ignite with a lightning strike. Firefighting equipment is overhauled and ready. Days become hotter and hotter till parched earth seems to hold its breath. Clouds build up each afternoon. "Yes, wind has been in the north a couple of days" – a good omen. The sky grows darker, clouds lower and flat bottomed. Lightning flicks wickedly against purple sky – the grass in contrast is almost white. Thunder rolls, shaking the house. Over there a curtain of rain hangs, another place sunlight glinting as your eye travels along the horizon. What is that? A white plume of smoke, or is it dust? A whirliwind? My heart skips a few beats hoping it is dust, but the haze is spreading. Blue-black now, the telephone is ringing. Someone else has noticed the smoke: hard to tell the distance, we take a bearing on it. Phone running hot - approximate location established. All stations are in gear heading for the fire. There is not much to block a fire with the wind behind it, despite fire ploughed tracks having been made during winter. A dry creek will slow the blaze, giving the men a chance to get it under control. Areas are large, the population small. There have been disasters when wind has suddenly changed - a truck caught and people burned. Planning and skills are highly developed and the power of fires respected.

During a lively storm it is not unusual to see several fires start up. On one such occasion when John and the older boys had gone to a fire on an adjoining station, a flash of lightning hit our Wirriadda paddock. Joe, about 9 or 10 years old, decided to ready the tractor with the Bromton rat. This is a V-shaped device, which hooked on the back of a tractor cuts a track; at the same time an attached drip torch, fuelled with a mix of diesel and kerosine, lights a fire which is drawn towards the bush fire by the vacuum created by the flames; thus a wide break is burned.

So here was little Joe manfully fuelling up and setting off to do his bit. John was returning when he met Joe. A few questions were asked. Joe said he had just put petrol in the drip torch - no diesel in the mix. It would have exploded had it been lit. Disaster was averted.

John had shown Bernadette how co-ordinates work, so, at first sign of fire, she would race to the fire radio to monitor the news while John hurried to fill the tank on the truck from the overhead tank. Doug Murray, fire captain from Glenlion station is on the radio "From here it's 107degrees south-west." He'd calmly state "What do you make of it Bruce?"
"Right." Bruce"s voice, a bit staticky from Carnwath station, "50 degrees south of south east."
"That places it pretty much on Maroola," Doug replies. Other voices chime in, plans made. Bernadette runs out to John with the location. It is as he thought by the smoke. He is giving orders:
"Conor you get this fuelled up while I grab the hand held." I am handing him packed sandwiches and a thermos.

Joe met with disaster years later in Townsville. An apprentice carpenter at age seventeen, riding to work on his motorbike, Joe collided with a truck. He sustained severe injuries. That day I was on my way to town. I had called in to Essex Downs to see Treen, my daughter-in-law. I remember exactly as if in slow motion - she walked out to the car with a look on her face which told me something was badly amiss. John was helping one of our neighbours muster so was out of contact. Unable to reach Bora on the telephone, Kimberley had rung Essex to tell of Joe's accident. It was as if I'd been thrown in a turbulent ocean with nothing to hang on to - and I'm not there for Joe, hundreds of miles away.

'What are the extent of his injuries?' Treen gave me a ray of hope. Kim had come upon the accident just as the ambulance left the scene. He knew instantly it was Joe's bike and followed the ambulance to the hospital. He caught up as Joe was being carried inside, looking a total mess.

'It's O.K. Joe, it's O.K." he stammered. You will be alright'.

'Bullshit, Kim!' Barely conscious, Joe replied to his brother. The sweetest words he could have heard, said Kim. He knew then, there was no brain damage. John and I drove to Townsville, being met on the steps of the hospital by Kim at 2 a.m. to be led to the intensive care unit. Joe slowly and bravely recovered under the skillful hands of orthopaedic surgeons.

All the children have stories of near escapes to do with motor bikes, common being encounters with snakes. Usually while tearing across the paddock to wheel a mob of steers or in a hurry to reach those wethers heading for the waterhole: There is a snake fair across the path. It is too close to swerve, too fast to miss. I have witnessed this, the rider literally rising into the air, legs outstretched as bike hits the ground further on, not missing a beat.

One Wet Season

We received the news that John's mother had died just after Christmas 1981. The worst time to leave home with the wet season expected anytime. There is no convenient time for a parent to die.

Hurriedly we packed and set off down the two thousand plus mile track to Sydney and goodbye to John's mother. After the funeral we left Matt at his new school, St. Josephs, and beat it back north. We reached Winton a couple of days later, anxiously watching the sky as we travelled. Surveying the north west towards home, still a hundred miles distant, the sky was positively threatening. John went to the Post Office to ring Ian Batt, our neighbour at Plainby and came back to the car. "Jump in everyone, we will head for Corfield and see if we can beat the rain." John had met Bob and Glenys Drury and two daughters who were keen to get to Richmond. Between them they'd decided we would travel together towards Hughenden to Corfield, a railway siding and pub. With luck we'd be able to cut across from there to Bora, and the Drury family to Richmond. Indeed Ian Batt had advised John not to attempt the direct route.

The plan worked well at first. We wasted no time hitting the road and made it to Corfield. By now the inky blue sky glowered over us. In the pub we met Bronc Steer who was about to head home to Kiriweena Station, on our road. Bronc in his Toyota led the way. Large drops of rain were kicking up dust. Soon dust was laid as rain bucketed down. Dirt turned sticky and dangerous, as John struggled to keep our vehicle heading in the right direction. At Kiraweena turnoff, it was clear we were not going to get much further, as we ploughed through inches of water, barely able to see through the swishing windscreen wipers. Bronc had stopped and was hauling chains from the back of his Toyota: "Here, hitch these onto the towbar John, and come in with me. I'll come back for Bob and co later." Bob's car had nosed into the table-drain and was there to stay.

So that was how we came to stay with Bronc at Kiraweena for ten days as a monsoonal trough drenched the Gulf Country.

Here we saw the phenomenon of raining fish. The homestead was on a slight rise surrounded by inundated paddocks and overflowing creeks. One morning the children came running in calling us outside. A heavy shower had just fallen and we saw little fish two and three inches long, flipping or dead all over the ground.

We took turns cooking, making free with Bronc's and Jan's wet season rations. Jan was away. Bronc, a raconteur entertained us. Chock-a-block with stories we sat around the table at night laughing. Bronc's telephone, connected to Corfield exchange, operated in daylight hours. The flood had however wreaked havoc washing telephone posts awry so that the line looped haphazardly, or dangled in water where supports were undermined. It became urgent to get communications working when Glenys, who had a condition requiring medication, was running out of tablets. The men and Brendan,* the oldest child, paddled for miles propping up posts, repairing the line

---

* *Conor and Kim had stayed with neighbours, Sean was working in the Northern Territory.*

as best they could. Contact was restored. A helicopter would be required to evacuate and this was arranged. We waited outside as the beating sound of the chopper approached. Bob, Glenys and the girls climbed in, lifted off and made a beeline for Richmond.

At Kirraweena, we heard no more for a couple of days till, out of the dark, Bob's footsteps clumping along the flagstoned verandah heralded his return. He had driven his tractor from Richmond to Sarre Station, walked twelve miles to Bora, fed the dogs and picked up our four wheel drive tractor, then driven sixty miles back to Kiraweena, leaving the tractor on the main road. The idea was that we would set off next day and go home on the tractor. In the morning Bronc had his rangy racehorse ready and loaded with necessary gear, he offered me a ride with Bernadette. I declined, not fancying the thought of trying to hold my baby as the horse plunged along. Walking through water and mud, steaming heat rising from waterlogged grass, Bernadette with plaster on her legs became heavier with every step. We reached the tractor with its carryall. Brendan, Quentin, Joe and Rosana climbed on leaning against the mudguards, then John, Bob, myself and Bernadette. That was enough.

We left Bronc and his horse, giants in an almost treeless landscape as our tractor chugged off issuing diesel smelling smoke. It took us all day, driving through water most of the time, the January sun beating mercilessly down, its hard reflections glittering into the distance. Thankfully though, the sturdy tractor didn't miss a beat surging through washouts while cutting deep tracks in the black soil. It was late afternoon when we reached Sarre where Audrey Bucknell had made us a tray of sandwiches. After our last lap to Bora the sun had sunk behind the stockyards. Oh! How good to be home.

SOTA - School of the Air

Educating children in isolated places is a formidable task. When searching for a property, I had requested somewhere within reach of a school bus, feeling I was not up to the challenge of doing the home-tutor role. On inspection, Bora offered such great possibilities that the 'school bus' idea fell by the wayside.

Before our formal correspondence lessons arrived, one of my nephews, who was travelling Australia, rolled up at our gate. Long-haired and barefoot in country where jeans and boots were order of the day, Gerard was a clever young man who had learned Greek at school just for fun. He agreed to teach our children for a period. Gerard's methods of teaching were as unconventional as his haircut, as he worked to instil an interest in classic learning in our bunch of brumbies. At the end of the day's lessons he would bundle the boys into his rattletrap car and drive a couple of miles up the paddock, then begin quizzing his pupils on the day's work. If the answers were correct they'd ride home in comfort, if not it was a hot dusty walk. To this day the boys can list off Australia's first six governors like a shot. After a time Gerard continued his travels towards greater things and I was thrown in at the deep end.

I had written to Queensland Education giving details of our school age children for correspondence lessons. Sean and

Matt were off to boarding school in Charters Towers, so that left Brendan, Conor, Kimberley and Quentin who was just starting. Four in a class doesn't sound many, but when each is in a different grade with an entirely different syllabus, the grade one child learning his sounds needing constant attention, the task is onerous. Rosana was still a baby crawling around and Joe, three years old, her protector. I made a point of giving them freedom of the classroom (within reason) so they'd not feel left out. Homemade play dough, butcher's paper and crayons were ever on hand.

Bora had a school room in which, before us, the Lord girls did their lessons. Marked on the door were measured heights of Lindy, Sue, Judy, Leigh, Erica and Jan and catching my fancy, in the pantry in childish letters was pencilled 'Erica is a pig'. Busy as life was, we had a set time to start school each day - stopping for smoko and lunch - at a fixed time as much as the men's work allowed. The normal subjects: maths, English, social studies, science and art were on the syllabus. L.O.T.E [languages other than English] were introduced by the time Rosana and Bernadette started school. A smattering of German and Japanese was learned. School generally finished about three o'clock, or when the work was done. That provided its own incentive to get on with the job.

In 1979 school lessons were mailed from Brisbane. School papers arrived on the mail in brown manila envelopes, and on completion of a fortnight's work was packed up and sent off for correction. Work coming back was embellished with purple printed stamps and comments. I enjoyed receiving notes of encouragement from the dedicated teachers in Brisbane, though we never met in person. Subsequently a long and happy association with Mount Isa School of the Air developed.

S.O.T.A. radio, with antenna and instructions how to install, arrived. John set it up on a tower, the aerial at right angles to the direction of Mount Isa. Now, both the papers plus the half hour 'on air' lessons came from Mount Isa. We had occasional visits from the itinerant teachers, much welcomed by the children and myself. They took over school for the day including fun activities such as shooting with bow and arrows; they would overnight with us before travelling on to the next station. We even had teachers arrive by aircraft, piloted by teacher Anne McGrath. Anne told me she had a fear of flying, so had faced it head on and learned to fly.

Originally S.O.T.A base was at Cloncurry, begun in 1960 after the Flying Doctor Service was founded by the visionary John Flynn. Bid O'Sullivan, a retired teacher, was brought back into service and she alone conducted the early 'on air' sessions for her scattered pupils. Peter Bucknell, who was our neighbour at Sarre was one of her first pupils. "It was exciting to have ON AIR lessons," he recalls "It was a change from having Mum or a governess teaching all day. To hear the voices from other places - there was Angus McClimont and his sister Penny from Maxwelton, Deb Keats from Maryron, and kids right out to the Territory". His voice changes "Of course wireless reception was erratic. Often we couldn't hear each other, or someone couldn't be heard, that was frustrating." Peter remembers Miss O'Sullivan as a very pleasant woman.

I can only imagine the task she had co-ordinating her one hour long daily class with children of all ages, whose faces she could not see. Budge Lillyman from Kara, north of Richmond was one of this group with his sister Gaye. "I didn't like it much, I was so shy". Then he laughs "But Gaye and I sung on air once. We sang 'There's a Hole in the Bucket.' for the ON AIR Christmas break-up concert". I have a card printed by the

I.C.P.A. (Isolated Childrens Parents Association). A child's drawing on the card depicts a country show, on the back the ten year old artist, Tim Hennessy, says "I am a fourth generation showman and I travel around with the show, my Grandfather and my father own all the joints and rides. Travelling around makes schooling hard but if it wasn't for correspondence, I probably couldn't write".

Our school day began when school notices were read over the school radio. I had to drop tools to listen for requirements for each child for that day. Requirements were generally simple e.g. exercise book, atlas, Cuisenaire rods. However on Fridays, I'd tear my hair at the teacher's creativity. It was art, craft and music day. The list for one child comprised a straw, a balloon (a scramble to find last birthday's candles - would there be a balloon among that?) For the next child, six bottles to be filled with varying amounts of water. Now, 'a collection from nature'. A feather? Send Kim to the chook yard. 'Oh no! Cooking!'

'What's wrong with cooking?' you may ask. Nothing – except when assembling the one and a half cups of flour, two eggs, melted margarine in saucepan and milk alongside the school radio. Add to that one eager child like Conor carrying out instructions over the radio – drop the wooden spoon to grab the mike – 'Conor, Conor with a question.' As a result, the scones or biscuits or pikelets, ready for the oven at the conclusion of the half hour, whilst embedded in the mesh of the speaker on the mike are wads of dough and the odd bit of eggshell. Next lesson, Quentin is on recorder. How lovely to have boys who appreciate music, giving them a rounded education, I wistfully mused. On-air music lessons I believe, had a unique style of teaching. The button on the microphone had to be pressed in when speaking or playing, but playing the instrument required two hands, so the mike was held between the pupils knees, which he pressed together when it was his turn to play. The system worked well, some children becoming proficient musicians - however a small brush with culture for my reluctant lot. Brendan's daughter is now learning the violin over the air – today they use telephone and computers with assurance.

Depending on whims of the weather such as sunspot activity, reception often was irregular. We got used to this and became quite expert at tuning in to get the gist of what was being said. A faint little voice may be heard cutting in and out, so that teacher at times had to guess - with sometimes funny results. A far off voice reports that his dog was bitten by a snake; after several attempts to hear the repeated message, the desperate teacher says 'That's good Tom. Good boy. Any one else with news?'

A highlight of the school year was S.O.T.A. sports and a seminar for home tutors. Mount Isa could be booked out, so it was a matter of booking the motel, then a flurry of packing, finding the yellow T- shirts from last year, for our family was in O'Sullivan team, blue T- shirts for Flynn. We would get a family-sized room at the Copper Gate. What luxury! It had a swimming pool and a TV (we had no TV at Bora). As we pulled into the parking space, other school of the air families in dust laden 4-wheel drives were arriving. I loved meeting up with other parents and governesses whom I'd got to know over the air waves. The seminars (in formal terms *professional development*) were organized by S.O.T.A staff. Karen Redman, in her years as head teacher, gave us many stimulating courses. We were introduced to de Bono over the air, on home tutor sessions, with his *Six Hat* lateral thinking. Kinetic, visual and audio ways of learning were talked about so that we home tutors would recognize, and better understand our pupils style of learning. For instance if he was a hands on kid, he may learn maths better by getting out the blocks (kinetic),whereas the visual learner would do well seeing reading and drawing.

In Mount Isa John was able to do the rounds of mining and spare parts yards picking up useful gear for Bora, a good bush mechanic looking on a scrap metal yard with a gleam in his eye. For me a welcome opportunity to check out the big shops of Mount Isa. On sports day John and the other dads helped set up tent shades and novelty races. Teachers were heard to say that S.O.T.A sports were the most uncompetitive in creation. Children were unused to ball games and the idea of having to win. Little kids in a race were just as likely to stop and wait for the others. We parents, with the responsibility of educating our children, the highs and lows that accompany this, as well as the vital question of how the season was going, built an unspoken bond.

Back home friendships continued. In later years Rosana corresponded with a distant classmate who sent her poems he had written, while Bernadette, out of school hours, would make a schedule on radio with Rachel to play noughts and crosses by numbering the squares.

Though I enjoyed the privilege of teaching my children, it was an all consuming responsibility. There were times, as the children rushed from the school room at the end of the days work, I would slump exhausted, thinking "I am an utter failure as a teacher. Yesterday I thought my child had grasped that concept, and now – it's as if he's never heard of it."

Oh well! When I met with other home tutors, we could get things in perspective. Nearly all shared these experiences.

I sometimes longed for the day when it would be all over. As it turned out, that burst of freedom soon evaporated when our youngest child, Bernadette, in Year 8, had to go off to boarding school. Her leaving home left a huge gap. Indescribable, the forsaken feeling in one's heart, handing one's child over to boarding school, while putting on a brave face for that child's sake - and lauding the exciting new experience ahead of them.

School of the Air

Shearing

Oh! The scent of a woolshed, of lanoline waxed wood
Witness to the passing of thousands of sheep.
Buzz of hand-pieces as fleeces peel off
Shearers with their unwritten law of fair play
Sharing pens, taking the good with the bad.

Smoko time,
Navy singletted shearers, towels slung over the shoulder
Sitting on wool bales savoring a mug of sweet tea.
Distant sounds of dogs barking, sheep bleating.

Under corrugated iron roof, mellow unmilled uprights
with a calligraphy of branding tar initials
decades of shearers gone by
History in branding oil.

Dogs leaping nimbly from woolly back to back
Dropping off in strategic places
to urge a recalcitrant old ewe onwards
as roustabouts hurry to keep catching pens full.

Familiar scenes repeated for shearing and crutching. The shed coming to life as shed-hands and shearers from as far afield as Tasmania and New Zealand or as near as the local town. Unheard of years ago, girls form an integral part of most teams; well travelled, plying their skills in Scotland, Ireland and the United States of America.

I cooked for the shearers for twenty-something years, at Cathedral and Bora, till my sons' wives, Treen, Sally and Lyn, relieved me of the responsibility. It helped me to make a list of meals before shearing, so there was variety in the meals. This also saved time, no thinking "What pudding for tonight?" Just go to it, apple pie, custard and jelly. Or main dish - Roast? No. Curry, with cold meat left from yesterday. Quantities of shearer sized loaves must be ordered from town to come out on the mail truck, this for smoko sandwiches, smoko being as important as the main meal.

Preparing breakfast was my least favourite. I would have to drag myself out of bed in the dark, fumble my way to the coolroom to get the heavy tray of chops or steak or sausages, cut up the evening before. By the time the shearers started trailing in at 6.30 a.m. to fill mugs with tea or coffee, the urn was boiling, chops cooked, onion gravy, and toast ready. I mustn't forget the black sauce! Worcestershire sauce was a must! Frankie flooded everything but ice cream with the stuff. As soon as breakfast was cleaned away and some beef or a couple of legs of mutton put in the oven to cook, there were sandwiches to be made for smoko at 9.30. and an orange cake (triple the recipe) put together.

Lunch of cold meat, salads and perhaps a potato bake, with fruit and cold cordial was demolished in minutes. The shearers were keen to get back to the shed to clean combs and cutters then stretch their aching limbs as they sprawled on the board for what was left of their hour-long break. Two hours shearing till 3 o'clock, smoko break, and at 5.30 the knock off whistle blew.

After showers with warm water from the donkey*, and a few beers, the shearers arrived for the evening meal, a much

Donkey: a hot water system made of a 44 drum over a fire, pipes etc. attached

more relaxed affair. Now all had more time to sit around the table talking. Through the day, family and whoever was on the staff, were in and out at odd times because newly shorn sheep had to be backlined for lice, branded and taken out to their paddock, while other mobs were being mustered into the shed and drafted.

It was shearing time when Cathy Freeman won her race at the Sydney Olympics. Around the Bora table all ears were tuned to the radio as that race was run. Then everyone practically erupted as Cathy won and did her victory round, flags flying. Cathy did some of her schooling at Hughenden. That night we claimed her as a local.

Stories of shearer's cooks, drover's cooks and station cooks abound. Andy Crawford, my nephew told me this one: He was wool classing at a shed in nor-west N.S.W. Normally, if not too far from town, shearers pack up on Friday after " knock off" and head for the nearest town for the weekend. On this occasion a couple of fellows from Western Australia decided to relax at the shed for the weekend, looking after themselves. When Sunday came round, Andy picked up the cook from Brewarrina and drove out the forty or so miles to the station. The cook was not in the best frame of mind, having been on the grog all weekend. Arriving at the shearers' quarters he tossed together something for the evening meal.
"We were all sitting round the table having tea," recalled Andy.
"There was a fair bit of banging of pots and pans and cupboard doors in the kitchen, then the next thing, in walks the cook and belts the unsuspecting W.A. shearer on the jaw."
"Why?" I asked Andy.
"Well, I dunno, I reckon he just didn't like the blokes using his kitchen when he was away. Cooks can be

funny. He was out of sorts alright. The contractor hadn't arrived and I was in charge, so I got up and gave him the sack. The West Australian bloke had a broken jaw. We were all a bit edgy. We could hear the cook in the kitchen noisily sharpening his knives. The situation was getting ordinary. Problem was I'd just sacked our cook and we had to have a cook"' Andy stated ruefully. "So I walked into the kitchen and said to old mate. 'Look come out here'." We walked to my ute and I said "I think we'd better talk about this in the morning. We'll settle it then". I reinstated him. He was sober in the morning.

From early days - when I began planning and worrying weeks before, organizing to take time off school to bake large slabs of fruit cake to be stored in the deep freeze, anxious to keep everyone happy - I realized I could look forward to the event. Over the years I gained confidence and regarded the team much as I'd regard my own children, two of whom were shearers for a number of years. It was a battle keeping space in crowded fridges for the all important beer. Sure, it was all early starts, but I was more organized during shearing than during the rest of the year.

Bernadette remembers, "Rosana and I were just ecstatic when Sean and Matt came home from shearing on Friday nights. We'd be watching for the lights." Lights in that open country could be seen for miles. "You'd see the lights and then they'd disappear for ages, and then you could hear Sean's old Toyota. It had a rattle." The boys made the most of it. "They'd get us to clean their vehicles. The deal was we could have any money we'd find in the car." A bonanza of dropped change. "They got us to clean their combs and cutters, and we carried their greasy 'dungers' (shearers' jeans – dungarees) over to be washed, all for a packet of lollies" laughs Bernadette. "It was so good to have them home."

Of course, there was always work lined up at Bora for when the big boys were home. A few extra hands to brand those calves, or muster Apple Tree and mark the lambs. Never a dull moment really, and no danger of getting lazy.

Cathedral

The 1980's proved to be a dry decade, more light wets than good seasons. Watching the feed, and predicting when we would need to 'lighten off' by selling stock if rain didn't fall by a certain date, was a constant.

With Bora dry, and carrying a fair number of sheep, the opportunity arose in 1983 to buy Cathedral Station. Seventy four thousand acres about eighty miles north west of Winton, we were very interested. Cathedral did not have a great reputation - 'out of the way, wild country' was the general local opinion.

The first time with the younger children John and I went to inspect it, we called in on Chris and David Batt at Nuken for a cuppa and a yarn. This became a habit over the years on the eighty mile cross country dividing Bora and Cathedral. We crossed the Diamantina and beheld in the distance Mt. Cathedral and the Cathedral Hills. I think we all fell in love with the place on sight. Up and down, over the tree lined channels of the upper Diamantina, mitchell grass came into view; beyond the undulating plains stood a line of olive green gidyea before the pink purple shimmering hills. Cathedral boundary was a high netting dingo fence. We drove along a winding track through gnarled gidyea scrub, negotiating rugged washaway gullies, out of the scrub onto red gravelly ridges - the coloured mesas, now in full view. There, the big old windmill and turkey nest tanks stood sentry to the Cathedral house and outbuildings.

Burke and Wills traversed somewhere near here on their fateful journey to the Gulf of Carpentaria. Just as a point of interest, Clio Station, between Bora and Cathedral, marks the watershed that divides the Gulf waters from the waterways that make their steady way to Lake Eyre.

We bought Cathedral for $6 an acre from Keith and Marge Montieth. Cathedral had been split off Dagworth Station when large stations were being cut up, allowing young people to get a start. Many of today's established station families started off in this way. 18-year old Mal Hosier won Cathedral in a ballot and built the house, originally to be shearers' quarters. Rooms opened onto gauzed verandahs with showers at one end. It became, and remained, the homestead.

Trucking most of our stock from Bora in the drought we ran the two places together. Back and forth a lot - vehicles loaded to the hilt, with supplies, medical kit, motor bikes, jetting trailer, lick blocks and ever present school work. In the 'build up' heat before Christmas we raced storms, or when a storm had crossed the road a nerve- wracking slipping sliding ride was in store for us.

Joining Cathedral is Dagworth station. Here Banjo Paterson, a friend of the owners in the 1890's, had written the words of *Waltzing Matilda* while Christina McPherson played the tune of an old Scottish hymn. Paterson's visit was soon after the shearers' strike, when the striking shearers were incensed at the graziers doing their own shearing at Dagworth. Conditions poor and feelings running high, Dagworth shed was burned down with sheep inside. It seems a feeble-minded man had been the culprit. He suicided. This sad story inspired our national song and was part of the beginning of unions in our country.

A poem written by Brendan:

To Waltz Once More

With conditions down and wages too
The shearers took a stand
To shear no more at the Dagworth shed
Till a raise was in their hand.

So strike they did; and strike a light
To the shed still full of sheep
And burnt it right to the ground
While the cocky lay asleep

The troubled soul who threw the torch
Was shamed by what he'd done
So turned the demons on himself
And died by his own gun

Out of work, and tucker too
The shearers stuck it out
A fair day's pay for a hard day's work
Was all they were about

In good time the winds of change
Blew slow but ever sure
Awards came in across the board
Till Matilda waltzed no more

We've come with haste down through the years
And things ain't been so bad
Through ups and downs we've ridden well -
For that we can be glad.

When mustering Cathedral we usually had an aircraft in the air. Both Damien and Brendan Curr, from next door at Dagworth, flew their own plane. It was a real benefit when one of them was available to fly as they were not only competent stockmen but knew the country. From the air, stock were spotted and buzzed, the pilot radioing to the musterers on the ground. Through the gidyea, stock would run out from a not yet dried up waterhole in those treacherous creeks or down the side of a spinifex-covered hill. Progress of the muster could be monitored from the house. I could hear the crackling voices when within range – then relay messages when those on the bikes were out of range. Now and then we'd glimpse the plane swoop down, skimming the trees then soar away out of sight.

The night before one muster, Duncan Fysh was staying overnight, his aircraft ready for a daylight start.* Quentin asked Duncan if he could ride in the plane. Duncan explained that it was his policy never to take anyone while mustering because all the ducking and weaving can very quickly bring on airsickness and he wouldn't have time to unload a sick passenger. Next morning the boys on bikes had set off before dawn to be at the back of the paddock by daylight. Duncan had gone to the airstrip, two miles distant to fuel up from the 44 drum of av gas.

At the time a roo shooter, Steve 'Bang Dead', was shooting on Cathedral. Working at night he would bring the skins to be salted and stacked in the woolshed. The younger children were up and about early when Quentin asked if he could take the Toyota up to the shed to help Steve. Joe and Bernadette hopped on the back and they set off. As I washed the breakfast

---

*Duncan is a nephew of the late Sir Hudson Fysh, a founding member of QANTAS. Hudson Fysh piloted its first flight which was from Cloncurry to Winton

dishes Joe came running home to announce that Quentin had broken his arm. No vehicles left, I ran up to the shed. When I saw Quentin, I had no doubt about the break. His upper arm was sticking out at a ghastly angle; and he was crying in pain. Driving round the corner of the yards, the rising sun had blinded Quentin, and he failed to see a solid stay-post standing a foot out of the ground; he drove hard onto it. The Toyota had come to a sudden stop, spinning the steering wheel which caught Quentin's arm. What to do now? Steve was not in from the paddock. No mobile vehicle – the Toyota was stuck fast on its stump. As best as I could I splinted and bandaged Quentin's arm, and leaving him with Joe and Bernadette for company I raced home to try and contact any of the musterers. All out of range! Kimberley hot footed it to the airstrip in the hope the plane would come in to refuel. Eventually I made contact with Sean who relayed the news on his radio.

Quentin was, after all, transported to Winton hospital in Duncan's plane. 'You'll do anything to get a ride, won't you mate?' remarked Duncan.

Gone Missing

Good news stories don't make news. Thankfully our lives are not spiced with too much drama - however I will relate one concerning Matt which happened soon after we took over at Cathedral.

It was Melbourne Cup Day, 1983. Sean had gone to Richmond, sixty miles north east of Bora, for the annual races. John and I were at Bora packing up to go to Cathedral the following day. Matt had been working at Cathedral for several days already. That night I rang Cathedral, intending to ask Matt if there was anything he wanted us to bring. There was no reply on the telephone. Puzzled, I left it a while and tried again with the same result. Where was Matt? Just to check, I rang Dagworth which was on the same party line as Cathedral. Carol Curr answered. 'Yes', she had spoken to Matt earlier in the day, and 'No' he had not mentioned going anywhere. Immediately my anxious mind began picturing Matt hurt somewhere on Cathedral – all seventy-four thousand acres of it. So easy to have an accident: a stack off his bike, or he had been scrub cutting with a chain saw. "Should be two people on those jobs" I was telling myself. Just months previously a station man, Chris, in the Richmond district, had come off his bike while moving stock, breaking his leg badly. (Unable to move, Chris had tried to send his dog home, but all the faithful dog would do was trot over to the bore drain 100 metres away, lie in it, have a good drink and pad back to Chris, shaking wet droplets onto the burning ground. It wasn't until evening when he hadn't returned that his family became alarmed. They alerted neighbours on the fire radio and a search was organized. It was midnight when the call was heard - Chris had been located. We held our breath. He was OK - hurt, but OK). These events, fresh in my mind, and vivid stories of people perishing in the heat did nothing to allay my fears.

Carol, bless her, assured me she would continue ringing Cathedral till she got Matt. Meantime Sean had arrived home. He was worried. John, in his practical way, was more inclined to think there was an ordinary explanation. Midnight now. Just then the telephone shrilled through the house. Carol – unable to contact Matt - had driven with her daughter, Miriam (their men were away) the fifteen miles to Cathedral. The shed lights were on – even the radio eerily playing music in the deserted shed. No Matt, and his bike was gone.

At this report John, Sean and I set off for Cathedral and at 2 a.m. were making search plans with Carol and Miriam. Mym had rung an agent in Winton to enquire if Matt was in town. 'No, he wasn't'. We didn't want to instigate a full scale search. Yet it was serious. John rang Duncan Fysh near Julia Creek, telling him the situation. He said he would come as soon as daylight permitted. We rang Batts at Nuken and Jeff Nichols at Bendemeer; both knew the country and would be with us for a daylight start. John, Sean and Mym, all experts at reading tracks, on motorbikes rode through the night searching for signs. No luck however. David Batt and Jeff Nicholson arrived before dawn and over cups of tea worked out a plan. The hum of Duncan's plane could be heard as the sky was just lightening in the east, the morning star aglow.

Carol and I held the fort at home, standing by the two-way radio in case Matt tried to contact us. He could be unconscious – who knew? We prayed. Stories of disaster crowd one's mind at such times. We decided to walk around the hills close by the house. We thought - the lights in the shed had been left on – could Matt have come home in the evening and seen a pig or a dingo and jumped on his bike with a rifle? So easy to stack a bike in those gullies. From up on the hills we heard a sound – a motor bike putt -putting towards the house. Not the searchers. We ran back. Matt, reasonably hale and hearty was climbing from his trusty bike and was much surprised to see Carol and his mother. He had, the evening before, decided to ride to the Blue Heeler at Kynuna, fifty miles away. It was, after all, Melbourne Cup Day - and Mum and Dad weren't coming till tomorrow. Our giggles of relief were a little weak. We got on the two-way to notify the search party that the lost sheep had returned.

It was a relieved group who now sat around the Cathedral kitchen making all sorts of threats to Matt. Duncan summed it up by saying they could chop him up and throw him out of the plane for dingo bait.

Cathedral Landscape

Tyler's Story

In a whirlwind the years pass. Our children are children no more. Working, travelling, studying, B and S balls, 21st birthday parties, leaving home, coming home with friends.

Sean was the first to marry, in 1990. He met Katrina, her smiling blue eyes reflecting the blue skies over Bourke from whence she came. They were married there by Father McGuire, who by this time was living back in Victoria. Judy Richardson, Katrina's mother, lived in Bourke and nursed in the hospital.

Sean and Treen, as she is affectionately known, made their first home at Cathedral. Sean was shearing at the time, with the Batt boys from Plainby. They had made up their own team, while carefully building up their stock numbers to carry on the tradition on the land.

At the gate to meet us now, when we went to Cathedral, was Treen, with the kettle on in the kitchen. She soon learned the run of Cathedral, able to check the waters regularly, a vital job. A burst water-line or broken trough can mean perishing cattle. No mean feat checking waters at Cathedral; the creeks presented a challenge. It went something like this: Into the four-wheel drive: Approaching the creek, shift into low second to drop down the steep bank on an angle, then hard right to avoid that big tree, just steady. Now, gun it like mad across the sandy stretch! For the steep climb up the further bank keep the wheels just so, to prevent getting hung up on that jutting bit in the cutaway. Treen took it all in her stride.

In early January, the onset of the wet season, Treen was expecting her first baby. With storms further upriver, the Diamantina (usually a network of dry channels) was running a banker a mile wide. The neighbours at Farewell Station, Rob and Jan Brown, were closer to the river so we would ring them if we needed to know what the river was doing. "It was running half a banka at Congewoy yesterday" we might hear, so we could estimate when the water would reach our crossing.

There was a worry about Treen's blood pressure so it was necessary for her to get to Winton for a check up. Rob Brown was a great one for machinery and had a collection of vehicles, including a hovercraft. Rob offered to hover Sean and Treen across the flooded river. There was a vehicle at Bendemeer Station on the other side. Piloting a hovercraft is a tetchy business; with Rob at the helm Treen had the ride of her life. They dodged coolibah branches as the unpredictable and hard to steer craft propelled them over the swirling brown waters.

Katelan, our first granddaughter was born in Bourke. She was Judy's (Treen's widowed mother)] first grandchild too. What excitement for our family! All uncles and aunts now, and so proud of the small Katelan, her eyes as big as saucers. Two years later, Tyler was born in Winton. He was soon a personality in his own right, climbing everything in sight - even the windmill one day!

Sean was offered the management of Essex Downs, thirty miles south of Richmond. Essex belonged to Americans, the big hearted Neal family. We knew them from their extended visits to Essex. Father and son had made local fame winning the roping event at Mt. Isa rodeo. Both Sean and Matt had spent time on Neal's ranch near Kingman in Arizona. Sean and Treen and children moved to Essex Downs with its expansive house surrounded by lawn and shady trees. It was situated half way to town for us at Bora, so we called in on our way whenever we went to town. So did others in the district - Sean and Treen's place has always been one of casual hospitality.

Now and then we would bring Katelan and Tyler back with us to overnight at Bora. On one of these visits I was bedding both down on a mattress in John's and my room. We were talking about what we would do in the morning. Painting, it was decided. Katelan took over in her 4-year 'older sister' organizing way, telling how she would paint grass and a shed and a tree. Tyler, feeling left out, asked in a plaintive voice "What can I paint?"
"You can paint the sky, Tyler" answered Katelan, never lost for a word.
"But Katelan, the sky is too high" complained Tyler.

Conor, a gifted footballer (till his knees were wrecked), had done his building apprenticeship in Sydney while playing footy. Back in Townsville he invited Sean to join his fledgling building company Windmill Bricklaying. This Sean did, relocating his family to Townsville.

This is where the accident occurred. Tyler, the little bush boy, ran out on the road and was hit by a car.

Just a 'phone call at Bora with Sean on the other end, with the dreadful news. Our world turned upside down. Tyler was in intensive care with head injury. John and I were in the car for the seven-hour drive to Tyler's bedside.

For the next five days our family haunted the intensive care unit at the Townsville General. Only two at a time allowed, keeping vigil by his bed. His beautiful little face with only a couple of scratches – just sleeping it seemed – though on life support. Drinking endless paper cups of coffee, we crowded the visitors' room, the smokers among us wearing a trail down the lift and out the back door, another meeting place, speaking in hushed tones. The image of a grown son, tears streaming down his face is branded on my memory.

Over these days Treen and Sean were inundated with calls of support - in love and prayers from friends and relatives near and far. A hundred times a day emotions rose and dropped with each new x-ray, even though we were not given hope by the doctors.

They were approached by doctors and asked if they would consider donating Tyler's organs. First response from Sean was "No way!". The idea of his son's body being invaded was too much. Days later, both Sean and Katrina had come to a different decision. Tyler's organs would be donated, to help others live.

Five days after the accident we gathered round Tyler's bed to say our goodbyes.

Our friend, Father Dave Lancini in St. Theresa's Church at Garbutt, officiated at Tyler's farewell. *Man of the 20th Century, Shaney Boy* and *Lord of the Dance* were the songs selected - even today these songs bring tears to my eyes. People from the west and Townsville were gathered for the funeral, overflowing the church. Instead of a black hearse, Matt had his Landrover ready to carry the casket which he, Kimberley and other family members had lovingly crafted. It had carved wooden flowers, his name and horseshoe handles. Tyler was familiar with riding in the back of trucks. He was carried by his uncles and placed on the back of the Landrover. Spontaneously they all climbed up, along with Rosana and Bernadette to accompany Tyler on his last ride.

*   *   *   *   *

Barefoot Kids

All my siblings and I are artistic in some way. We were encouraged in this (as long as our efforts were original – "No copying" our father instilled in us). On rainy days we would run outside, find sticks and draw enormous pictures on the damp ground. Free and uncomplicated. 'Children draw from the heart' it is said. Through school and beyond I painted and drew pictures, unable to leave a tidy margin in my exercise books. This love has remained with me, enhanced by various schools along the way. Memorable was Doug Navo, flamboyant postmaster at Quambone telephone exchange. When we came back from W.A., Doug was holding weekly night classes at the school. A group, young and old, was instructed as he opened a new world of possibilities in paint. Later in North West Qld, I joined the Flying Art School, brainchild of Mervyn Moriarty. Tutors periodically flew to isolated towns where art enthusiasts collectively travelled hundreds of miles to paint together.

While teaching correspondence school I noticed the pained expressions on the faces of my early learners as they stumbled their way through Nip and Fluff and Dick and Dora of the beginner readers' books. Dick and Dora were neat suburban children in shoes and socks, pictured on manicured lawn as they greeted their father who held a brief-case and wore a TIE. I longed to create something that outback children could relate to.

As the idea grew my enthusiasm blossomed. After Tyler died I worked on a children's book dedicated to his memory. Barefoot kids with wide-brimmed hats, mud cakes, horses and cattle. A labour of love, drawing on life experiences. My watercolour paintings of children of the outback illustrate this publication titled *Outback Alphabet.*

At the time, Marie Mahood, well loved throughout the outback, and our friend since Balgo days, was launching her book *Crocodile Dreaming* in Winton's Waltzing Matilda Centre. She generously invited me to launch my children's book at the same time. It was an exciting event for me, especially as my first batch of books arrived at the last minute per kind favour Mac Air (also instituted in the outback). Seeing the shiny cover with the image of our four eldest sons on it, and flipping through the coloured pages I had laboured over gave me butterflies. That Sean and Quentin drove many hours to be there, and back home through the night, touched me. Marie, John and I reminisced into the night.

Colin Munro on A B C's *Summer All Over* interviewed me. True gentleman that he is Colin, intuited my nerves before recording. He put me at my ease "Forget that you are on air, and the people out there, just talk to me." It worked. His background knowledge of the country and his skill asking the right questions brought forth a flurry of letters and phone calls. I got busy filling in invoices and mailing out books. My relief can be imagined when the cost of self publishing was covered, and better. Numerous letters from all parts of Australia came, the writers sometimes sharing their own experiences. It was both humbling and a delight. *Outback Count Out* followed and now Boolerong Press has taken over publishing. I have written and illustrated a children's story *Grandma's Precious Chest* and illustrated a book of Australian Songs.

Surely, I feel that Tyler, our little angel from above, has had a hand in it all. I decided to put a proportion of the sales towards the Fred Hollows Foundation which has done so much for isolated people everywhere.

A Patchwork

Full years, busy years,
A patchwork of days
Of nappies flapping in the sunshine,
Always a baby on my hip and
one tugging on blue jeans asking something.

Infant gurgling in his cot, Next
on his dad's knee helping steer the truck.
In no time we are lifting him
Onto the back of the truck-
The back of a horse.

Scratched knees- stuck in the burrs,
Making jelly, coconut ice, hot cross buns.
Child crying enough to break my heart
Five minutes later, laughing with abandon
Tears forgotten.

Ah! If only we grown ups could do this.

Amidst the hurly burly of family we parents endeavor to instill consideration for others and responsibility. Out mustering cattle one day, I became aware that my growing children were looking out for me, instead of the other way around. Four or five of us were on horses or motor bike, "Mum, I'll take the Winchester boundary. Give me a bit of a start, then you pick up anything I turn in, keep them going towards the creek. By then Brendan and Sean should have a fair mob together and they can hook up." I was instructed to take the easier part to muster while my children took on the more difficult. No longer had I to scan the distance to catch sight of my child to see if he was managing. Something of a milestone. I breathed easy.

'Quality time' is a phrase often used. I think *any* time is quality time in the ordinary everyday stuff of life, clothed in love. It doesn't always seem so 'Quality' when sitting with a sick child, or reprimanding him or her. But surely it is in the *being there* through thick and thin that builds quality? Under John's uncompromising eye and my protective wing, our children have grown up with a healthy respect for work. There were times I felt it was all work and little play, but John's example of hard work, and ability to improvise to make things work, has stood them in good stead.

The rhythm of station life carries on, accepting the seasons as they come. There is reward and satisfaction in seeing a good crop of calves through weaning, branding and educating them. They are transformed from a mob of young things as ready to run over you as around you, to docile animals.

A young Aborigine was working with us as a ringer a few years ago. He and I were taking weaners to their paddock. Task almost completed, I rode back from the lead as the mob fanned out. Malcolm ambled up beside my horse. "There's not a prettier sound in the world, Eh! Mrs.Kersh!" I paused. Dry grass rustled as cattle contentedly moved through it, heads down. "So true Mal," I agreed. "It is a beautiful sound. Dry grass whispering".

So many rewarding years of hard work, making ends meet, successfully running Bora and Cathedral. John did not rest. He was constantly innovative - whether selecting or culling sheep to grow a finer micron wool, or in landcare, or in politics. Ever on the go, the stresses must have caught up with him. He had a breakdown. We know now that this is not uncommon: One out of five people suffer bouts of depression at some stage of life. To see someone who was so much in charge of things, seemingly so confident, suddenly at a loss, was dismaying.

It was at Easter time, when multitudes had gathered at Bora for the christening of two of our grandchildren, that John told me he was not able to handle things. With the help of our friend, the local doctor, a specialist was lined up in Townsville to see John. So he went back to Townsville with Sean and Katrina. After consultation, medication was prescribed. It was a horrible time for John. He had a series of anxiety attacks. This was shocking to me because John was normally the very opposite of anxious. It was alarming for him to meet this onslaught.

At home I carried on, maintaining the routine. Most important seeing that waters were in order, fixing a bore drain broken out, water running away and stock in the next paddock doing a perish. Or checking those nearly dry waterholes on the creek where stock insist on hanging, and bogging, even though they have been moved to the trough a couple of times already.

Over this period, Matt, who was running his own business in partnership with his brother Kimberley, offered to come out to Bora to help keep things going. He, his wife Lyn, and their two little boys came out and, like a duck to water, Matt got straight into organizing the crutching.

John came home, and for a time was housebound, happy to let Matt take the reins. That was uncharacteristic as well – but here was a different John, able to lie in bed as I read the paper to him, and even willing to talk about what was happening for him. We considered selling Bora and going into a joint grazing operation with Brendan and his wife Sally. By the day of the auction, however, we had cooled down on this idea. Luckily the bid didn't make our reserve price.

After a time, things got back on track for John, health wise. Brendan and Sally made a decision to buy Cathedral and eventually Matt and Lyn leased Bora.

Sadly, after thirty-nine years of marriage, John decided to go his separate way. Being a "separated wife" happened to other people – this was too close to home. It was not the way it was supposed to be, I thought. Grandparents should be together – let alone parents! Ideally… Together we had had an exciting journey and were privileged to know wonderful people along the way. Life takes some strange turns. There is always something new to learn on the road ahead.

Separation was a challenge! At the end of this dry year there was no sign of wet and no early storms. Bora was carrying big numbers of sheep and some cattle. Decisions had to be made. To feed stock in hope of a late wet? Or cut our losses and sell? Stockfeed from the south was all but unobtainable. In former times we had transported high protein lupin seed from N.S.W. but none to be had now, the south was dry too. Prices had skyrocketed. Matt found someone on the Atherton Tableland who had Rhodes grass hay bales and corn for sale. It was on its way. Mid January now, we would feed for the next six weeks, and if rain had not come, off-load then.

Grazier's life is a constant gamble, an educated gamble. Plenty of times people sold stock at give away prices, gave delivery and the long awaited rain came only days later. "Lucky for the other fella, that's the way it goes. Next time will be our turn". Gamblers and philosophers…

Matt and Lyn were to take over in a couple of months. During the intervening time I moved from the main house to the cottage nearby (part of the station complex of shed, yards etc.) and looked after Bora. Different members of the family came for vital jobs like mustering, drafting, preparing mobs for sale and delving the bore drains. Brendan and Sally at Cathedral were a constant support. Conor brought his tiptruck to feed out corn and hay; this truck had a flat top with tipper at the back so was just right for the task. Matt was back and forth from Townsville. He was transferring his business to his brother Kimberley. My job was feeding the stock, checking waters. Troughs, bore drains – and rapidly drying waterholes in the creeks, death traps for stock.

Extract from diary:

Jan. 29 *Checked pipe (bore drain crossing) in Dimora, it was blocked - water held up, cleaned rubbish out. Balgo drain drying up. Went back this evening (20 mile roundtrip) to check, water has gone through corner Apple Tree almost into Balgo. Drove to Woolerina and Bore paddock, cleaned troughs, sheep into hay o.k. half eaten. Bernadette arrived from Longreach 7.30 p.m. Hot day 40 something.*

Jan. 30 *Took feed to rams. Bernadette and I put lick blocks out for cattle. Bore water now flowing well into Balgo.*

Rosana arrived back from America. It was a blessing to have her home for a time to share the responsibility, her slim artist's hand competently changing the six forward gears in Conor's truck, negotiating winding wheel tracks down a creek bank, careful to avoid an overhanging branch. At the sound of the truck sheep came running across the scorched paddock, forming a long curve as they found the grain, bowed heads, and gobbled. We drove round in a large semi circle lifting the tipper at an angle to let go a stream of corn, enough not to be lost in the dust, but not too much to allow sheep to gorge themselves and bloat. A fine balance. The hay bales had to be rolled off the side of the flat top, the enclosing mesh cut off with an old butcher's knife, and spread out. Rhodes grass is cattle feed, unpalatable to sheep, but with nothing else available we found the sheep chewed it out of necessity.

Sometimes I felt I was carrying the drought on my own, watching the stock. Were they keeping their strength up? Or pulling sheep from a bog in a dried up waterhole, then trying to get them to stand up to get them to water. Splattered in mud, and worn out I note a lone crow, statue still on a coolibah, eyeing the sheep patiently. So discouraging I want to cry. A visit from a neighbour, or the mailman coming brought light relief when we could share our woes or even a joke. Still I couldn't prevent myself from examining practically every tussock of dry grass to see if I could conjure up a green shoot. This is when I realized more than ever how dependant I had been in many ways. Always relying on John and the children being so capable. Since they were little our children were eager to fuel up a vehicle, put air in the tyres or fix a puncture. They had learned these basic skills early and I was out of practice.

Each day the hay had to be loaded onto the flatback of the truck. The nerves in my stomach churned at the thought of the bobcat, a tough old yellow machine. Climbing up I had to drop a steel bar across my lap before the motor would start, a safety device (guaranteed to give confidence!) then push this button, pull that lever and it would spring into ear shattering life. Next, drive it into the shed and line up the forks in front with the 200kg round bale, drive forward to spear it with forks at a slight upward tilt so the bale won't slide off. Lift, and back out to place bale on truck, tipping fork forward till bale slides, then back off. The second layer meant lifting the bale above the height of the bobcat. The delicate part of the operation, because if the bale was not carefully balanced the bobcat became cantankerous. In fact it seemed to become as nervous as me, its driver. It went into a bucking motion which almost made me lose my senses, so I could forget which button to push or lever to pull or whatever, all the while the hot noisy motor belching diesel fumes around me. Wiping tears of helpless frustration from my eyes I would climb off, weak at the knees. "I cannot do this, I'm too little." The job had to be done, however, and I could do it. I would tackle the wretched thing again, and gradually my confidence built.

Through the years I have received many blessings, my greatest joy being my children. I am so grateful for them. Each is so different and each one a gem. Independent, generous people who contribute in ways I cannot begin to list or even know. I am grateful, too, for my daughters-in-law who have introduced threads of other family cultures to weave into ours, expanding our horizons. And grandchildren, what gifts! They sparkle in their variety.

Life in rainbow colours turns like the fan on the wind-mill, faithfully drawing its life-giving water to revitalize body and spirit.

Epilogue
My Beautiful Wild Son

The world has just turned over, or has it stopped? Those words Sean just spoke make no sense.

"Mum, Matt has been killed".

"No! Sean, stop it!" my mind is screaming. Conor, Treen, Kimberley and Sean - a tableau in Sean's and Treen's kitchen. What are they doing here? There's a thundering in my ears. None of it makes sense. Sean is holding me or I'll fall into a thousand pieces.

It is two nights before Christmas Eve, 2008. I am here at Sean and Treen's place in Townsville, ready to go west on the bus in the morning, to Richmond where Matt will meet me. It is all planned: To share Christmas at Bora with Matt, Lyn, the kids and Lyn's parents, Pat and Bruce. My bag is packed, isn't it? Full of presents wrapped in pretty paper for the family out west. Minutes ago, my only concern was how the large painting for Brendan and Sally would travel on the bus to Cloncurry.

Conor is talking. Matt, Lyn, their children, Jai, Zade, Mackenzie and Pipi with Lyn's parents this evening went to Sarre, twelve miles east of Bora. A Christmas get-together with neighbours.

"The kids, playing with a kite. It got caught on the power line". Conor continues "Matt on the forklift of the tractor to fish the kite off. The power must have jumped".

Like stones in my heart the heavy words are dropping. Tears, men crying, my sons. Not Matt, he couldn't! It is a bad dream. What a cliché. *A nightmare* doesn't even begin to describe it.

They tried for an hour to resuscitate Matt. The ambulance and doctor from Richmond arrived at Sarre. Nothing could be done. Matt had died instantly.

Quentin, Sandy and then John came in to Sean's. Jason, Matt's neighbour and friend (who was in Townsville) walked into the kitchen, hugging us, sobbing. Big tough Jason. Joe, thankfully, was back from Dubai. Rosana had to be told. And Bernadette, on duty tonight at the General. Brendan was already on his way from Cloncurry to arrive at Bora at 3 a.m. Some of us were to drive out to Bora in the morning.

The following days run together whilst organizing Matt's funeral four days after Christmas. The telephone is running hot with loving messages. Neighbours come over and put chocolate cakes in the deep freeze, leave a bottle of wine. Hope for early storms had not eventuated, just the odd shower here or there.

There were some bright spots over this sorrowful time. Friends of Lyn and Matt passing through spent an hour and more in the horse yard with the boys. We all gravitated over there to watch through the rails. This horseman, Scotty, was a joy to watch, as he quietly instructed with Zade's newly broken-in horse. It was as if he had all the time in the world, even though he and his family had a good six-hour drive ahead of them. Zade hung on his every word. Both he and Jai then had a ride to demonstrate what they'd been learning.

Mackenzie, who was eight and Pipi, seven years old, and I decide to go in search of some flowers for a bouquet. There is a plant which grows in the wet season and dries out with seed pods opening into cream shell-like petals. Hand in hand we walk along the track towards the shearing shed. Mackenzie and Pipi every so often run to pick up a pebble or dry bit of grass that catches their attention. A pair of eagles soar effortlessly overhead. I am thinking of Matt. Pipi says out of the blue, "Daddy's not really gone you know." I stop.
"How do you mean, Pip?" I ask.
"Well, he's in here," patting her heart.
"He will always be here," her beautiful brown eyes reflective. Out of the mouths of babes.

My brother Mike who travelled up for Matt's funeral wrote an account in his local paper. I quote part of it here:

Richmond Church was never going to be big enough so the proceedings were moved to the Racecourse where quite a few still stood in the sun. Richmond is a small country community that has in recent years developed a degree of pride in their town. They built a lake visible from the main street. They renovated the old convent for community and a spiritual centre. Generally the town is not showing the years of drought that has wearied a lot of small communities.

Matt was credited with being one of the movers and shakers who got Richmond revving and they came to send him off in style. Some five or six hundred attended his funeral.

His brothers built him a coffin with a verandah on each side, with a ripple iron roof and *Bora* painted on the roof. His brothers and mates spoke of the times they had shared. Then for a hearse they used a station truck, a large contingent of the family travelled to the cemetery on that truck, with Matt escorted by three Harleys ridden by Sean, Joe and mate Jed McCoy, with Matt's sons Jai and Zade as pillion passengers.

The heavens opened at the cemetery. All were drenched. They lowered Matt to his final resting abode with bronco ropes that were left with him. The members of the family then left a variety of symbolic things with him. This was particularly moving when his son Jai picked up his bogeye, (shearing handpiece) gave it consideration, and then put it in the grave.

By the time we had returned to town where friends had made their home available we were dry again. We then had the opportunity to meet some of Matt's friends and some of our own family that we don't often see.

Christmas, New Year and family go together. I had the priviledge of being part of Matt's funeral and farewell. Strange but true, the privilege was being part of a funeral of a young fellow leaving a young family behind. As Christians we believe that death is a temporary separation so a funeral should be a celebration of life mixed with the sadness we all felt. And so it was.

* * * * *

We arrive home to Bora the day after Matt's funeral. That night insects in their millions come in every crack and cranny, the gauze, it seems, no barrier. Lights are turned off to discourage the invasion.

The next night the 'Wet' started, crashing thunder tearing the humid stillness. Sheet lightning illuminates bedroom walls. I hear the first heavy drops on tin roof - then down it comes. All night it rains, thunder rumbling off into the distance.

Morning reveals a landscape transformed. Sheets of water across paddocks reflect a close grey sky. Plainby, Belford, Dundee - the phone is rejoicing. No local storm, this is monsoon rain. All have had inches overnight. "And more to come," gleefully forecasts Harry from Plainby.

Mckenzie and Pipi in singlets and shorts are running, slipping and sliding along the track, thoroughly muddy and loving it. Jai and Zade find an old boogy board to take to the creek, running waist deep through the cattle lane. I watch as they take turns being swept along in the current till pinned against the fence on the other side. They wade back to repeat the performance, wet hair plastered down and shouting, wholly absorbed. Thank God for this respite. I am starting to think we can only take so much sadness at a time, that some protective wall holds back the dam of tears in us.

A week later Pat is taking the little girls to Brisbane. I will go to Townsville. Dan Flute, a helicopter musterer from near Richmond, Matt's friend, will ferry us out. With very minimum of baggage I climb into the chopper. Mckenzie climbs onto my knee. Dan shows me the strap which I wrap round us both. Pat and Pip will come on the next trip. Dan, barefoot, revvs up the chopper and lifts off, clumps of mud dropping from its feet.

It is my first ride in a chopper. I have one arm round Mckenzie the other hand clutching the edge of the Perspex. Mildly terrified, I am determined not to show it, as Dan casually remarks on the scene below. There are no doors on this machine, the wind whips my jeans and my darling granddaughter grows heavier. Water! So much of it! From this perspective it is hard to recognize where we are, bore drains lined with prickly acacia look like creeks, little mobs of cattle bunched together, or a cow and calf on an island, their tracks making patterns on the sodden black soil. There is no mistaking Alex Creek as it comes into view; it must be half a mile wide. We begin to look for the road leading to Richmond.

* * * * *

My mind travels back along the years. Matt was the first in our family to travel overseas. Destination Arizona, starting a procession of his siblings.

The Neil family owned Essex Downs in our district, a family concern. Also a ranch near Kingman, Arizona; they were indeed a pioneering family in that area. Matt celebrating his 21st birthday with John T. Neil, the same age, at the Neil ranch.

Driving around the ranch one day, Matt spotted a wild creature running through the desert brush.
"What is it?" Matt wanted to know. John T. said
"I'll race you to catch it." Like a flash both were out of the pickup running. Matt, good at most things, could run alright. He was the first to dive on that black and white ball of fur. You've guessed it, it was a skunk and John T. was standing back, hands on hips laughing.
"The stink was unbearable." Matt reported "I had to toss my clothes out."

As he was leaving the States, Matt was loaded with presents for home: A teddy bear for Rosana, which had a red heart with a light that switched on and off; a teddy with blue overalls and wheels for Bernadette; exquisite Indian turquoise and silver jewellery for me. No one was forgotten. For his younger brothers, wild looking knives with compasses on their handles. These did not go un-noticed at the Los Angeles airport. The authorities pulled Matt out of the line and ushered him to the security room.

"What are the knives for?" they wanted to know.

"To kill things" Matt replied.

Wrong answer! It would probably get him in real trouble today. At any rate they soon realized Matt was a genuine bush article, and no danger to world peace. They became friendly, and were interested to hear about his Australia.

*   *   *   *   *

Cascading like a stack of cards memories crowd by - Matt on a bike pulling up beside Jai or Zade, Jason, James or Rob, hats casting shadows on their faces, legs outstretched as cattle move together into a mob, brown yellow and grey stitched onto swathes of creamy grass. Bucking out of the chute, one hand in the air, the other firmly grasping the monkey strap at Kynuna rodeo, tang of beer and aroma of sizzling steak mingle as the crowd yells encouragement. Matt, sure to be one of the stayers sitting round a fire at 6 a.m. after a party, becoming more wise and philosophical as night turns into day.

There was that time Matt surprised us, with a four-wheeler motor bike, the first in the district. Unloading it on the bank of the dam, before reaching the house, delighting his younger siblings as they watched him roar up on this new-fangled

machine. Soon all were competing for the first ride. Soon after, on a muster at Cathedral, out at the Bowgunyah tank having lunch.
"Fair dinkum. It is supposed to float on water too", he told us.

Too good a chance to pass up, Matt and Sean thought they would see if this was true. So with the tyres well pumped up, Matt guided it down the bank and into the expanse of muddy water. It churned along the top for about five metres then began to sink, boys in pursuit to rescue the heavy sinking machine. Sean explained that air in the tyres has to be a certain pressure, after that the air becomes weight. Matt, in his inimitable way, if something's good, more is better, had pumped the tyres to full capacity.

Matt never complained. Just after he left school a government agent rang. Matt took the call. There was to be a meeting for the youth.
"We wish to discuss issues with the young people. What the problems are" said the earnest voice on the telephone.
"There are no problems" Matt summed it up. That was how he saw it. Straight forward and uncomplicated.

I am thankful for the five years I had living in the weatherboard cottage when Lyn and Matt leased Bora. It is an immeasurable privilege knowing my grandchildren who freely came and went between the main house and my place. Mackenzie and Pipi carrying the yellow plastic bucket to the chook-yard to feed the chooks, two or three assorted dogs traipsing behind them. Zade on his motor bike telling me just how you balance as you do a wheely, or Jai discussing some of the big questions over an early morning cup of tea.

Lyn in the evening, brown hair pinned up, watering her loved garden, an oasis she had created out of the relative desert I had left her. Matt on the phone at daylight,
"Are you ready Mum? Come over for a coffee." The morning star hanging just above the horizon, before an early muster.

About three weeks after Matt died, Bernadette sent an e-mail round the family. She had found an emu egg Matt had given her about five years ago. I quote Bernadette's note: "I have moved about six times so the fact that the egg is still intact is a minor miracle. When I read the words, I was sure Matt had wanted me to find it yesterday and let me know that its OK. Here is the poem that he lovingly hand carved for me:

I hope my achievements in life shall be these-
That I will have fought for what was right and fair,
That I will have risked for what will have mattered,
That I will have given help to those who were in need,
And that I will have left the earth a better place for what I have done and who I have been.

Norah Kersh Jan 2010